MEN WHO HATE THEMSELVES

And The Women Who Agree With Them

DAVID A. RUDNITSKY

BOOKS

A Division Of Shapolsky Publishers

Men Who Hate Themselves

S.P.I. BOOKS
A division of Shapolsky Publishers, Inc.

Copyright © 1990, 1994 by David Rudnitsky

ISBN 1-56171-276-0

Previously published as a trade paperback by
New American Library, 1990

Revised and updated S.P.I. Books edition, 1994

For any additional information, contact:

S.P.I. BOOKS/Shapolsky Publishers, Inc.
136 West 22nd Street
New York, NY 10011
212/633-2022 / FAX 212/633-2123

Manufactured in Canada

10 9 8 7 6 5 4 3 2 1

CONTENTS

4

ALSO BY THE AUTHOR

1001 WAYS YOU REVEAL YOUR PERSONALITY*

1001 MORE WAYS YOU REVEAL YOUR
     PERSONALITY*

THE JOY OF DEPRESSION

LOVE CODES*

PARENTS WHO STAY LOVERS*

THE SUPERSTAR WORKOUT**

DIONNE! THE AUTOBIOGRAPHY OF
     DIONNE WARWICK***

*with Dr. Elayne Kahn
**with Rob Parr
***with Dionne Warwick

DEDICATED TO:
THE MEMORY OF
SAM RUDNITSKY

Who taught me to love words and wonderful
books, and whose intelligence, kindness, and
gentle sense of humor will always live on.

ABOUT THE AUTHOR

Born out of gridlock, in the backseat of a taxicab, Mr. Rudnitsky shares his birthdate with Helen Keller and Attila the Hun, explaining why so many of his contemporaries consider him a deaf mute barbarian. During his early years his mother diligently attended to the household and, by age 39, he no longer needed to be breastfed.

Mr. Rudnitsky (that's Rud-Niet-Ski, Russian for condominium) is a popular figure at seminars and lectures across the country, with his notorious sense of humor frequently provoking audiences to near riotous states of total absence.

Even at family gatherings relatives often force him to dodge questions—and occasionally a brick. On the plus side, close associates find him a modest, unaffected person, who recently underwent emergency liposuction—on his ego.

In real life Rudnitsky is Creative Director of one of the largest advertising agencies in all of Sri Lanka. Ask anyone in the business and they'll immediately tell you that his award-winning commercials have electrified millions upon millions of bacteria on TV screens from coast-to-coast.

Currently, the author is writing on an inspirational new work that will encourage Americans to give up their dreary nine-to-five jobs and, instead, pursue the exciting, fast-paced life of a writer of humor books.

Coming Soon:
POVERTY WITHOUT RISK

CHARTS IN THIS BOOK:

MEN WHO HATE THEMSELVES...

By Size of Penis
By Favorite Rock Group
By Father's Occupation
By Country
By Exercises They Hate
By Exercises They Love
By Favorite Sexual Fantasy
By Girlfriend's Bra Size
By Visa Credit Limit
By College Major
By City
By Favorite Pet
By Favorite Movie
By Favorite Author
By First Name
By Wife's First Name
By Favorite Food

1

WOMEN WHO WRITE
TOO MUCH

Across the country, wherever you go, from north to south, east to west, even outside Cleveland, more and more men are beginning to realize how much they hate themselves.

Of course for some it required that their consciousness had to be raised with a tow truck, but for most others it was a natural outgrowth of the women's movement of the 60s, 70s and 80s. Indeed, before the Gloria Steinems and the Betty Friedans, most men never dreamt how selfish, petty, and hostile they really were.

Well, all this has changed. By 1993, sociologists predict that almost all men will hate themselves. In fact, if current trends continue, only one man will be able to successfully love himself by the year 1999—and that will be, according to all indicators, Donald Trump.

AMOEBAS, PARAMECIUM, AND INSURANCE AGENTS

When you add up all the pages and all the books that have helped to teach men how vile and loathsome they really are; when you add up the collected works of Shere Hite, Robin Norwood, Germaine Greer, etc., etc., etc., you have over 7,885,612,943,221,112,637 words which have been exclusively devoted to making men feel as if they were below the amoeba, the paramecium, or even some insurance agents, on the evolutionary scale.

Contrast this to all the positive words these women have written about men and you will quickly see there have only been about 11, and most of these have dealt with the superior ability that men exhibit when it comes to moving pianos.

TARRED, FEATHERED, AND FORCED TO APPEAR ON GERALDO RIVERA

Clearly, the problem isn't "Women Who Love Too Much", but "Women Who Write Too Much", who are responsible for the millions of men who hate themselves today. However, should a man ever dare to articulate this point of view in public—just see how long it is before he's tarred, feathered, or even worse, forced to appear on the Geraldo Rivera show.

Why men never before realized what sleaze they really are is still a mystery. After all there are countless reasons to hate oneself. A man can be too short, too tall, too fat, too thin; he can be losing his looks, the hair on his head, and even more traumatically, the hair on his chest. So when you look at the over-all picture there are literally thousands of good reasons for men to hate themselves.

Which brings us to another significant point. How many men can really find reasons to love themselves? Let's face it, even the historically strong points of the male animal have been turned into negatives by the powerful Women's Movement.

STOCKBROKERS, LIBRARIANS, AND SERBIAN BODYBUILDERS

Take for instance a stockbroker who occasionally works late, some weekends, and who only earns annually about $875,000 or so. Well, before you know it his wife is accusing him of having tunnel vision, of being too "focused" on money and therefore not "sensitive" enough to her needs. So he quits his job, becomes a part-time librarian, and what do you know? The very same woman accuses him of being a spineless wimp who'll never get ahead anyway and guess what... she winds up leaving him— for a macho Serbian bodybuilder!

COMPASSION, UNDERSTANDING, AND A SIX PACK OF BUD

Small wonder from northern Maine to southern California men are showing how much they hate themselves. They're letting out their feelings, as well as their pants, and what are they getting in return? Nothing. Nothing but threats and accusations, warnings that they will lose the one thing they love more than anything else in the world, unless they pay up their American Express bill.

Has anyone, anywhere, heard their cries for help? All they want is love, softness, compassion, and understanding, OK, maybe with a six pack of Bud thrown in.

THE HIGHEST STATE A MAN CAN REACH (WITHOUT GRASS OR COCAINE)

The highest state a man can possibly reach today is "accepting" himself, which doesn't do most women any good since most of these types of guys are probably gays anyway. So what's the answer?

If current census figures are to be believed, there are exactly 125,834,917 men living in these United States today and even more, over the past 50 years, who have died. When you add these figures up, there have been over 300 million men who have inhabited this nation at one time or another, many of whom had the good fortune to enjoy the unique benefits of male bonding, which in some cases kept them out of the army.

THE EVOLUTION OF MEN'S FEELINGS:

In the year 234,879 B.C. (that's Before Consciousness), men were a pretty happy lot, content to eat brontosaurus burgers at their leisure. Clubs for men also existed, although these were frequently used to beat women into submission. But did we hear any complaints? Obviously not. Those were the good old days!

THE STONE AGE, THE BRONZE AGE, AND THE AGE OF MAKE-UP

Moving along a few hundred thousand centuries we arrive at the end of the Bronze Age and at the start of the Age of Make-Up. Perhaps the best known figure of this time is Cleopatra, who seduced Marc Anthony with her wit, charm, and Humphrey Bogart imitations, all the while unconcerned that she was tying up important commercial barge traffic up and down the Nile.

A few hundred years later and the Romans are still having a grand old time conquering neighboring lands. They plunder, steal, rape, pillage, and sell short. But instead of castigation and cries of misogyny from the various women's groups of the time, they are rewarded with laurel wreaths and weekend passes to Sodem and Gemorahville.

INFIDELS, WITCHES, AND MONDAY NIGHT FOOTBALL

Anyway, the Roman Empire ultimately falls which ushers in the Dark Ages. Here again, even though all learning and civilization have practically disappeared, men are still pretty much a happy species, torturing heretics, fighting infidels, with occasional time off for burning witches and Monday Night Football.

Once more, do we hear any complaints from the women? Of course not. They're too busy treating plague victims to be bothered with petty issues like day care, abortion, and the inalienable right to pick up the check—once in awhile.

THE HISTORY OF WOMEN'S OPPRESSION OF MEN:

The very first example of this, according to historical records, has to be Delilah, the cunning wench who cut off all of Samson's hair, even though he only came in for a light trim. Next are the Sirens of Greece who decide, while at the beauty parlor, not only to drive men crazy with their song, but to play havoc with the damn ferry schedules as well.

And through all of this, speaking of driving men crazy, let us again turn our attention once more to Cleopatra, a woman so manipulative, so ruthless, that she eventually had Marc Anthony kissing her asp.

14

Cleopatra forces Marc Anthony to kiss her asp.

QUEEN ELIZABETH, QUEEN ISABELLA, AND NANCY REAGAN

By the Middle Ages, a time so named because almost all the men in the world were between 40 and 60 years old, women practically dominated the globe. Queen Elizabeth, Queen Isabella, and Nancy Reagan—all had hundreds of servants and men-in-waiting at their beck and call.

With one stroke of the pen, they could declare war, imprison thousands, and reduce prices on carpets by as much as 15%. These were powerful, influential women, whose decrees and dictates could not be questioned—even by Oprah Winfrey.

OVERSEXED AND OVERWEIGHT

Which brings us to the Renaissance, where Rubenesque women were seen everywhere, mostly because they were so large. In fact many of these women carried enough poundage to be awarded with their own zip codes and, it was not uncommon, to see hordes of men erecting moats around them.

A little later on came Joan of Arc, a popular singer whose big hit "Smoke Gets In Your Eyes" helped catapult her to one of the most powerful positions in France. And speaking of powerful French women, what about Josephine, who not only showed Napoleon how to conquer Spain, Germany and England, but also how to make love to her—without falling off.

BY THE 20TH CENTURY WOMEN DOMINATE THE GLOBE

Except for a few Islamic countries where men can still have members of their harem burned at the stake, beheaded, or even slowly tortured to death—by Bobby Vinton records.

Shere Shi'ite (author of "The Shi'ite Report") recommends broad economic sanctions against these countries but fails to address the larger issue: what if these same Arab states, in retaliation, decide to cut off our country's vital supply of high-grade, Sin Similyan halvah?

THOROUGHLY FABRICATED CASE STUDIES

In this book we will look at all the reasons that men hate themselves. We will offer charts, facts, figures and thoroughly fabricated case studies. But beyond all that we will document the women who hate these men as well.

Indeed, to protect the integrity of this book's conclusions, and to justify the big advance we got from our generous, crazy publisher, we've conducted out own in-depth survey and found out some pretty interesting facts. For instance, of the women we queried, only 93 million confessed to actually loving men, but of course their testimony had to be totally discarded, for the sake of accuracy.

A MAN WHO NEGLECTS HIS WIFE, CHILDREN, AND HIS SIDEBURNS

Through the following chapters, we shall detail all the signs that positively identify a man who hates himself, who neglects his wonderful wife, his lovely children, and especially his sideburns—all dead give-aways for a sick, sick puppy. We will show what men who hate themselves eat, what they wear, and how they style their hair. Moreover, we will give specific physical descriptions of them, their height, weight, and if they have any, their depth.

And as if all this weren't hateful enough, we will interview the women who make it a point to hate

17

these awsome men. We will delve into who these women are, where they came from, and how we can get them to go back.

A TEN POINT RECOVERY PROGRAM—FOLLOWED BY A TEN POINT RE-UPHOLSTERY PROGRAM.

On top of all this, *Men Who Hate Themselves* will offer men around the world a ten point recovery program and, after that, a special bonus ten-point re-upholstery program.

One last thing: Before we proceed there may be those of you who assume that the author, for whatever reason, is acting out of a peculiar form of misogyny. Well, let us assure you, nothing could be further from the truth, as you will find that he's quite happily married and has a wife and child in Connecticut, a wife and child in North Carolina, not to mention his other wife and child in Tibet.

2

LOVE, MARRIAGE AND PRE-MARITAL DIVORCE

Much of the information in this chapter comes from a detailed questionnaire that we mailed across the country to men and women of either sex. And the results were quite intriguing. Actually the results could have been even more intriguing, had we remembered to enclose our return address. But that's neither here nor there.

One of the leading reasons we found out that so many men hate themselves is because of their complex sexuality, and boy did we hear about some complexes! 12% of the male respondents admitted that they could only be sexually aroused during group sex, although many of them ultimately confessed that the closest they had ever come to group sex in their lives was by masturbating with both hands.

LEARNING THE FACTS OF STRIFE

But we uncovered facts even more surprising. For example, almost all the men we spoke to felt strongly pressured, after dining alone at an expensive restaurant, to go home with themselves.

Of the women, only a mere 14% of those who responded were female, but they quickly pointed out the reasons they hated men as well. Fully 56% of the women hated men who found it difficult to maintain an erection, and an apartment in New York City, at the same time. However, of these same women, 67% admitted to the fact that they were over eighty years old and still using a diaphragm, but only when they lied about their age.

WE ASKED SOME VERY PERSONAL QUESTIONS

1. Do you ever achieve orgasm through manual stimulation and, if there were no Manual around, would you consider a Carlos or a Raul?

2. Have you ever had sexual feelings towards your brother? Sister? Your podiatrist?

3. Do you believe in "Open Marriage," and if so, how late do you stay open?

4. Have you ever been a celibate? A halibut?

5. Who usually breaks up the involvement first? You? Your lover? Or the police?

6. When you fall asleep do you review the day's events in your mind? Or do you let Siskel and Ebert do it?

7. In order to stop you from "clinging" to them, have your lovers ever used Static Guard?

8. Have you ever used a dildo to reach orgasm? A dill pickle?

9. While making love, do you prefer touching your partner with tenderness? Or with gloves?

10. Do you engage in long and protracted foreplay? Fiveplay? Sixplay?

11. To arouse the person you're with would you lick then slowly at bedtime? Or quickly at Parchisi?

12. Right now, do you have a regular lover? Have they ever been constipated?

This chapter is entirely based on the responses we received to these questions, from places as far away and as alien to the human mind as Nebraska. But sophisticated though we thought we were, the survey uncovered forms of sexuality heretofore unknown to us. For instance, this response from Beverly Hills:

DIDN'T LIKE "CONVENTIONAL" SEX:

"The woman I lived with for over eleven years couldn't achieve orgasm in the conventional way, so she stopped going to conventions. But that wasn't the most disturbing part of the relationship.

"What really ticked me off was that she found shopping more of a sexual release than any she could have with me. As a matter of fact, at Bloomingdale's, particularly during half-price sales, she would achieve a full and satisfying 'storegasm.'

"Suffice to say, after returning home, this quite often resulted in her being unable to have sexual relations with me because—she claimed—that she was totally spent. This went on and on until finally, after much agonizing, I decided that I could no longer live with a woman who was 'Buy-sexual.'"

'Buy Sexual'

And we received this response from a man who preferred that we didn't use his name, but identified himself as a recent Democratic candidate for the Presidency of the United States.

BLATENT CUOMOSEXUALITY

"My wife would only get excited when I dressed up a certain way, preferably to resemble the governor of New York State. Even then, the only way to make sure that she really got excited was for me to stand by the bed and recite the keynote address to the 1984 Democratic convention. Sometimes I had to do this two or three times. It gradually began to dawn on me, and this wasn't easy to accept, that I had married a latent Cuomosexual."

THE MYTH OF THE MALE ORGASM

Obviously, this was a man who had minimal confidence and esteem. So little, as a matter of fact, that he always felt obliged when he was with a woman he really liked, to fake erection.

Time and time again, as seasoned and professional as we thought we were, we were shocked by the revelations we heard in the private suite at Motel 6 that we had rented for our interviews. There were moments when we wanted to flee from the room, scream, cry—but only when the movie channel was showing Rocky V.

GENTLEMEN, GENETICS, AND GENITALS:

Our research got into other interesting areas as well. We discovered there was an interesting correlation between how much a man hated himself and the size of his genitals.

For instance, a carpenter from Topeka was so well-endowed that he was given fifteen years in prison for raping a stewardess on an American Airlines flight, even though she was 28,000 feet above him at the time.

Another man, an employee of the telephone company, had such a small organ that he received a special grant from MIT to participate in a study that sought to prove the existence of imaginary points. A study that was subsequently successful, but only after six months of research which led to the discovery of his penis through an electron microscope.

WOOL BLANKETS, HORSE BLANKETS, AND SECURITY BLANKETS

To present our findings more thoroughly, the following chart represents the evidence that we uncovered. Let's see, altogether we uncovered 439 men sleeping under wool blankets, 972 men wrapped in horse blankets, and 26,801 men hiding beneath various security blankets.

For the sake of accuracy we made every effort to accumulate these figures as quickly as possible since, in the act of uncovering, the cold air was likely to diminish our measurements. This became pitifully obvious, 400 miles north of Juneau, when we removed the blubber comforter of an eskimo. Unfortunately the poor soul not only lost his erection, but his penis had to be immediately defrosted for 20 minutes inside a microwave.

MEN WHO HATE THEMSELVES: BY SIZE OF PENIS	
1/4" or less	100+%
1 1/16"	99.4%
2 3/4"	92.8%
3 1/4"	82.1%
3 1/2"	81.9%
4 5/32"	74.2%
5"	60.3%
6"	50%
7 1/100"	5.1%
8 1/4"	1.7%
9 57/93"	1.0%
Over 10"	0.0000000003%
Over 15"	No data available*
* researcher still in state of shock.	

PENIS FIXATION AND HOCKEY PUCKS

Finally, of all these men, 4% were fixated on their own penis, 3% were fixated on someone else's penis, and 93% were fixated on a hockey game. But clearly, the most unexpected finding of all was that 99.7% of these men were also schizophrenic and allegedly reported that, during masturbation, they experienced simultaneous orgasm.

THE RELATIONSHIP BETWEEN WOMEN & MALE MASTURBATION

Most women though, were clearly uninterested in the process of male masturbation, unless they had a headache that night. What concerned the majority of them was the tenderness and understanding that a man brought to the most intimate act known to human beings and his willingness, after climax, to take out the garbage.

ORALLY, MANUALLY, AND FINANCIALLY

Without a doubt women from every economic and geographical sphere agreed that men were almost completely ignorant about how to excite them in the ways they most wanted, whether it was orally, manually, or most important of all, financially.

The following case study is a common example of what we heard:

DOUG, DORIS, AND HER CLITORIS

"During the first ten years of our marriage, Doug had a hard time finding my clitoris. First he looked under the bed, then under the pillow, and once he even dug up part of the front yard. Finally, I overcame my embarrassment and told him exactly where to look. You should of seen the shock on his face!"

SEXUAL POSITIONS AND IMPOSITIONS

High up on women's complaint list were men's preference of sexual positions which, from their point of view, were really sexual impositions. Because of cultural role models and deep feelings of insecurity we discovered that most men preferred to be on top—on top of the dresser, the refrigerator, anywhere but in bed.

Most men prefer being on top—of the dresser!

SETS HER BIOLOGICAL CLOCK THREE HOURS BACK

Without a doubt, one of the driving forces behind women's anxiety was the feeling that time was running out to find Mr. Right. Nanette DiComo of San Francisco was so distraught over this that it took twelve years for her therapist to finally convince her that her biological clock was really on Eastern Standard time, meaning that she had an extra three hours to meet a man. Unfortunatly Nanette, who was quite petite, also had a habit of meeting a whole assortment of men who were absolutely wrong for her. Here she recounts a recent blind date with Louis Vanderschmeer, the world-famous mosquito trainer:

AN IMMENSE SEXUAL APPETITE

"Louis had an immense sexual appetite. Well actually, he had a sexual appetite for women who were immense. He shunned any female who tipped the scales at less that 400 pounds and indeed preferred women who could not only tip the scales, but the Queen Mary as well.

"He was fond of coming over to his lady friends' homes, picking them up with a crane, and then chauffeuring them around town. I heard his last affair ended tragically when the women of his dreams broke his heart, by sitting on his chest."

*Ernie's wife got so fat that it broke his
heart, liver, kidneys ....*

MOST MEN AREN'T SUITABLE

Again and again, we heard of women finding out that the men they were going out with weren't suitable; in fact some of them weren't even capable of putting on sportsjackets. "It's hell," says Michaela Jackson of Savannah, Georgia. "All the men I meet are into short term relationships. How do I know? Because most of them are on Death Row."

It's the kind of situation Samantha Bupkes is quite familiar with. Beautiful and gifted, with degrees in electrical engineering and optometry, Samantha won a Nobel prize for discovering how to cure glaucoma in electric eyes. Yet as attractive and talented as she is, even Samantha has remarkable trouble in finding a man who is truly on her level:

STAN, DAN AND THE TOBACCO LOBBY

"You know, Stan didn't exactly have the greatest grasp of contemporary issues. He heard Dan Rather talking about the tobacco lobby and thought it was a place where you go to smoke.

"OK, let me tell you about his last girlfriend Sheila. Now I wouldn't exactly say that she was promiscuous but, in her high school sex education class, she was voted 'The Most Likely to Conceive.'

"Oh Danny, Danny, you know I really lowered my standards to date him, since he was about 2'5" tall."

THE TRUTH ABOUT THE MAN SHORTAGE

Samantha's relationship brings to light another critical issue, the man shortage, primarily caused by the glut of men who are short. Short men are everywhere you turn, but you can't see them, unless you also happen to be searching the sidewalk for some spare change.

Naomi Mendez of Peoria only found her fiancé after accidently stepping on him. Janet Fishbein rescued the man she lives with from drowning through the use of her quick wits and resolve, not to mention her dexterity with a bathroom plunger. Finally, there's Maxine Putro of Baltimore, who came home one summer's day only to discover that her husband Bernie had run off that afternoon and eloped— with a gerbil!

The Man Shortage

31

IS BIGGER REALLY BETTER?

But let's not assume that it's merely short men who hate themselves. Tall men are every bit as prone to hating themselves as well. (Here, we define tall as any man who can peer down and see Wilt Chamberlain's bald spot.)

Wilbur Butte of Atlanta requires a tractor just to drag his mittens along. Ollie South of Buffalo can't even limbo under a football goal post. And Jed Dubonk, from Montreal, was recently hired by NASA to retrieve defective satellites—with his hand!

Clearly, it's easy to see why these men feel they stand out in a crowd. And that's why in most social situations they feel the awkward need to crouch down—especially when talking to God. On the plus side, tall men are usually taken more seriously than short men; even more so when they're threatening to destroy your condo with their big toe.

MEN WHO HATE THEMSELVES: BY FAVORITE ROCK GROUP

The Beatles	01%
The Rolling Stones	01.1%
The Rolling Papers	01.11%
Black Sabbath	99%
White Sabbath	98.9%
Beige Sabbath	97%
The Jimi Hendrix Experience	50%
The Jimmy Carter Experience	500%
The Four Seasons	04%
The Four Tops	04%
The Four Skins	89%
The Jackson Five	17%
The Jesse Jackson Five	17.7%
The Police	28%
The Cops	28%
Huey Lewis and the News	09%

3

EARLY ADOLESCENCE
(THE DEFORMATIVE YEARS):
AGES 6-81

Protracted adolescence is quite a common occurrence among many men and there are numerous reports of those, well into their 70's, who report their first pubic hair. Cy Napse, a whiz kid at age 65, still enjoys dipping little girl's pigtails into inkwells. But just because Cy has the maturity of a nine-year-old child, don't assume that this has hampered him in the business world.

For after school he's actually a major financier whose skills at mergers produced "The Washington Post Cereal Company," an outfit that enjoyed considerable success the moment it started marketing a new type of Shredded Wheat, one in the shape of Col. Oliver North.

Yet despite his material success, Cy recalls an early childhood incident that brings tears to his eyes. Either that, or he has a serious allergy.

SHE HAD THE FACE OF AN EIGHTY-YEAR-OLD WOMAN

"Once, after my mother brought me home from school, I remember my father screaming at her at the top of his lungs, "I can't stand it anymore! You have the face of an eighty-year-old woman!" Yes, I remember the entire incident quite clearly, even though I was only sixty-five at the time."

Cy attributes the stormy relationship between his parents to his feeling that all relationships eventually become suffocating, particularly if your lover is holding a pillow.

WILBUR KAPUTNIK'S PATERNAL PROBLEMS

Of course there have been some men who have been even more directly persecuted by their fathers. Wilbur Kaputnik, a distributor of hole foods, such as doughnuts, bagels, and Life Savers, recounts his father's stern treatment of him:

HIS FATHER BEAT HIM EVERYDAY—AT GIN RUMMY

"My father used to deliver threats, ultimatums, and yes, even pizza—he was that kind of guy. An exceptionally cold and brutal man, he used to take me out behind the woodshed everyday and beat me—usually at poker, but occasionally at gin rummy as well.

"As you can see, he was a very disturbed person. I remember how he would force me to make my bed and then, after I did that, he would force me to make dressers, drawers, and once even a vanity table."

AND MOM RAN OFF WITH A PROFESSIONAL SWORD SWALLOWER

"He hated everyone. And things didn't improve any when my mother ran off with a professional sword swallower.

"But when I look back, I feel sorry for him. He really was a bitter, isolated man, whose only joy in life seemed to come from listening to an obscure piece of classical Chinese music, entitled "The Nutcracker Sweet and Sour.""

A COMMON THREAD

Apparently, one of the things that Wilbur was most ashamed of was his father's occupation, and this turned out to be a very common thread among Men Who Hate Themselves. By carrying out exhaustive research that lasted through most of our sushi platter, we were able to isolate those paternal careers that produced these feelings of self-loathing, we think.

MEN WHO HATE THEMSELVES: BY FATHER'S OCCUPATIONS	
Anchovy Trainers	23%
Volunteer Arsonists	39%
Anvil Salesmen	51%
Water Bedouins	7%
Loincloth Repairmen	32%
Piano Mover and Shakers	44%
Stuffed Dermatologists	88%
Bushmen (Appointees of George Bush)	371%

MEN IN THE PRIME OF THEIR SENILITY

As this chart clearly indicates, early parental influences affect both men in the prime of their life, as well as men in the prime of their senility. Quite often, mothers and fathers don't mean to be cruel, but try explaining this to Phil Bopski of Cleveland, who remains bitter to this day because his parents put powdered milk in his baby bottle.

BRONZED HIS BABY SHOES— WHILE HE STILL WAS WEARING THEM!

Or to Regis Grillox of Houston, who remembers the day his parents bronzed his baby shoes—while he was still wearing them. Even today Regis struggles to come to terms with his emotions, but while he's made them a good faith offer, it looks like he'll still be forced to arbitrate.

For a period of over five years, we collected data. We received thousands upon thousands of letters and this one is fairly typical of those we threw away.

HIS FATHER BURNT HIS BRIDGES BEHIND HIM

> "When I was growing up, my parents moved around a lot, but they never left me a forwarding address. It's not surprising. My father was the type of man who burnt his bridges behind him, his caps, and he once even tried setting fire to his root canal work.
>
> "Still, I know that I really loved him. The man was sixty-five years old and had the incredible body of a twenty-year-old swimmer, although he never seemed quite capable of locating the head."

FEAR AND LOATHING IN MILWAUKEE

"I remember the day we moved to Milwaukee. That was where they sent me to this private school. What a place! The nuns would give me incredible beatings everyday—which was kind of strange—since I was attending a yeshiva.

"Yet when I look back, I realize a lot of things that I didn't appreciate before. Sure, my parents could've spoiled me, but that would have first meant taking me out of the freezer."

WHY PARENTS SAY: KISS MY ASSETS!

Probing the male psyche deeper and deeper, a number of things became plainly obvious. All too often there was unfinished business between men and their parents and, no matter how hard they tried to reason with them, most parents still refused to put all their worldly assets in their son's names. Jordan Rivers, of Kalamazoo, shows us that a wealthy upbringing can be just as damaging as a poor one.

THE TITANIC AND THE BOSTON HERBAL TEA PARTY

"The neighborhood where I was brought up was so affluent that we fought our gang wars with mercenaries. But despite this, dad had a rigid personality, so rigid that mom often used him as an ironing board.

"It was a strange childhood. You see, my father never got over the fact that my grandmother went down on the Titanic—but as we later found out, she did the whole crew."

THE BOSTON HERBAL
TEA PARTY

"Instead, he preferred to trace our family history back to the days of the American revolution when our ancestors proudly instigated the Boston Herbal Tea Party, successfully turning the entire harbor and parts of Martha's Vineyard the color of Red Zinger.

"It's true. With my father just the thought of Christmas and family was enough to warm the cockles of his heart, but if that didn't work, we made sure to put a hot plate across his chest."

PRE-MED, PRE-LAW,
AND PRE-FETUS

In addition to parents, siblings can have a significant effect on how little a man thinks of himself. Dudley Schmendrake of Wichita Falls recalls that his older sister Ruth was pre-med, his younger sister Elayne pre-law, while they treated him like a pre-fetus.

"You could register their hostility towards me on a seismograph," he asserts indignantly. And when you examine the record there's absolutely no doubt that Dudley's speaking the truth, quite a rare thing for a man, since it occurs about as frequently as an ice age.

According to his recollections, Dudley's sister Ruth used to play very cruel tricks on him. She once told him that when he was born there was incredible confusion, with the doctors spending most of the afternoon and much of the evening slapping each other. The story made Dudley burst into tears—on his 35th birthday too!

VANISHED DURING LIPOSUCTION!

By all accounts a miserable woman, sister Ruth was a compulsive eater who was to mysteriously disappear in Europe during emergency liposuction. From then on, the only trace of her was a faint voice emanating from the tip of a straw.

But sister Elayne was a much different story. An obsessive personality, she always insisted on watering the plants before leaving the house, even though they were all artificial.

THE POPE, THE BOSTON MARATHON, AND REEBOKS

A mere fifty-five years younger than Dudley, he still recalls her vividly. "I can even remember her favorite book," he says with a grin on his face. "'The Jogging Shoes of the Fisherman.' It was about the winner of the Boston marathon who, through a strange twist of fate, becomes Pope and excommunicates anyone caught not wearing Reeboks.

To this day Dudley truly believes that Elayne was

secretly enamored of him. Well, upon further study into his childhood, we think that perhaps enameled is a better word, since she was always cementing little tiles all over his body.

THE UNCONSCIOUS MESSAGES MEN RECEIVE FROM THEIR MOTHERS (USUALLY ON THEIR ANSWERING MACHINES)

"I'm sick and tired of talking to a machine. Aren't you ever home? Where are you? Out all night with some floozy! Just like your father! When I was the one who worked all day and all night to put you through—(BEEP) I hate that beep!

"Do you know how much this call is costing

me! A lot you care they're forcing me to share my oxygen tent with a family of kangaroos. I hate Australia! Why you sent me here I'll never-- (BEEP) That beep is driving me crazy! Is that your plan? To drive me crazy. So that you can inherit the Kaiser's invasion plans? Never! I'll take them to my grave with—(BEEP)

"Why aren't you there? Wasn't I always there for you? That's right. Who put up your bail when you were convicted of playing canasta with an underage panda? Me, that's who. But do you— (BEEP) Tell me, is playing the spoons a living? At least you could try playing the knives and forks as well. Oh I don't know—(BEEP)

"I remember when you used to come home from embalming school, the smell of Aqua Velva on your breath, and I was so proud of you. Such a-(BEEP) Good boy. Such a nice boy. Such a— (BEEP)—Such—(BEEP) Su—(BEEP BEEP BEEP) Listen I know you're— (BEEP)"

THE UNCONSCIOUS MESSAGES MEN RECEIVE FROM THEIR FATHERS (USUALLY ON THEIR ANSWERING MACHINES)

"Hey, can I spend a few days over there. Your mother is driving me crazy!"

MOTHER SUPERIOR/FATHER INFERIOR

The above profile is a classic case of a parental relationship which is referred to, in professional circles, as "Mother Superior/Father Inferior." Men Who Hate Themselves are frequently the product these kind of troubled unions.

A clear example of this is Herbert Schismo of Ft. Worth, who recalls that every night his mother would repeatedly strike his father, often carrying a picket sign until her demands were met.

WHY MEN ARE A DIME A DOZEN

Yet even before she married his father, it was clear that she had a negative view of the opposite sex. "Most of the men I've met are a dime a dozen, which is highway robbery," she would say. "Even taking into account the rate of inflation." An angry, frustrated woman, why she married his father (an alcoholic musician capable of playing only in one key—whiskey) remains a mystery to this day.

Once Herbert tried to broach the subject of his father with his mother. He pleaded with her to be more tolerant by arguing that alcoholism was just a disease. "Oh yeah," she retorted. "Think I was born yesterday. Next thing you'll try and tell me is that cancer is just a disease too."

Obviously, she was a difficult woman. And due to her influence, Herbert has always felt compelled to impress his dates by making sure he takes them to the fanciest restaurants in town. Places so expensive that its almost always required, when you order the house salad, to take out a mortgage.

Today, the memory of his mother and father still haunts Herbert. But there's one moment, in particular, that he'll never forget:

HERBERT TALKS ABOUT HIS HORRIBLE LOSS

> "Look this is not easy to talk about. I experienced a horrible loss the day both my parents died in that car crash. Yes, I remember it all quite clearly. Because I had bet on the Yankees to win."

The next chapter picks up on this important theme. Providing we can figure out, by then, exactly what that theme was.

MEN WHO HATE THEMSELVES: BY COUNTRY	
France	01.1%
India	04.3%
Zimbabwe	28.5%
Yugoslavia	47.2%
Italy	00.0%
Canada	50.2%
Thailand	02.8%
Germany	93.4%
England	93.5%
Tahiti	00.7%
Brazil	02.9%
Brooklyn	87.6%
Denmark	14.7%
Japan	00.1%
Syria	06.7%
Israel	07.6%
United States	105.9%

* Actually, the figure was even less.

4

MEN WHO SHOULD HATE THEMSELVES, BUT DON'T

Men of any age or economic group, and this is not widely known, can also suffer from PMS (Pre-Marital Syndrome), which usually strikes before asking any woman for a second date. So before calling again they wait a little while, customarily five or six years, in the hope that the woman will go and seek another lover—preferably one in Bangla Desh.

Now while there's every reason for these men to hate themselves, most of them don't, although they might occasionally chastise themselves by nicking their faces with a razor. But no matter how they justify themselves, the effect that men afflicted with PMS can have on women is all to often devastating. Take the case of Abigail who...

CRIED HERSELF A RIVER

"After my last boyfriend left me, I stayed in bed for a month and cried myself a river, although since I lived in Boston, the river was soon polluted and I was eventually fined over two million dollars by the EPA."

MISOGYNY AND MAURICE CHEVALIER

Yes, misogyny expresses itself in many ways, but rarely in the music of Maurice Chevalier. Quite often it's displayed by the lack of concern men seem to have for the women they're involved with. It happened to Gloria Estabar of San Salvador, when she broke off her engagement to a leading Nicaraguan rebel, after he refused to use a Contra-ceptive. Here's another example of how men vent their rage:

HE WAS GOOD AT EXPRESSING HIS ANGER—IN LATVIAN!

"Mark was very good at expressing his anger, but it never did me any good, since he usually expressed it in fluent Latvian. I will admit this though, he did have a talent for getting things off his chest, especially the chest of drawers I once put on it.

"Day after day he would throw one tantrum after another and, when he ran out of tantrums, he would throw TV sets, toasters, I mean the guy really terrified me. Especially when he did his Shelley Winters imitations. I don't know.

"Things deteriorated quickly and he started calling me lots of names—stupid, incompetent, and once even Seymour Mendez, though I never found out why. I guess the last straw was the night we went to a very expensive French restaurant where he insisted on splitting the check—with an ax!"

Splitting the check.

TONY WAS FULL OF BALONEY

Another category of man who should hate himself is the vain, self-centered type, like Tony. Sharon first met him on the set of a Hollywood film—where she had a job as the director's chair. At the time Tony was starring in a new sci-fi movie in which a tiny little Mexican, wearing a sombrero, explodes out of his chest. The film was called "Illegal Alien."

49

WHY TONY DECLINED BEING A CENTERFOLD

"Tony was this incredibly sexy guy. In fact this women's magazine came to him and wanted him to be their centerfold, although he later declined when he found out where the staple would go. But despite the fact he was strong and virile, he was also withholding. So much so, that I thought I was entitled to a refund.

"Listen, I tried to improve the situation. One night I placed a copy of the Comma-Sutra (that ancient sex manual for High School english teachers) on his pillow, but he became completely impotent. It took me three weeks to explain to him that syntax was not a special charge the government put on oral sex."

"IT WAS GOOD FOR ME. WAS IT GOOD FOR I?"

"Yeah looking back, I suppose the guy was really only concerned with himself. After we were through making love he'd turn to me and say, "It was good for me. Was it good for I?"

"All in all, when you come to think about it, I would have to say that Tony was pretty self-centered. A few weeks after we broke up my friends told me that he went to a doctor who only treated people with incredible egos. An "I" doctor, I guess."

SHE PROPHETED FROM HER EXPERIENCE

Soon after this relationship Sharon underwent a complete change. She became a spiritual being and—in just six months—did EST, turned into a Hare Krishna, and then married and divorced the Maharishi Yogi. Suffice to say, for tax purposes, she's now computing a Prophet and Loss statement.

THE MOST HEINOUS COLOGNES EVER CONCEIVED

A substantial majority of the women we spoke to felt that you could count all of men's good points on the fingers of one of Venus de Milo's hands. Time after time they cited instances of incredible cruelty and abuse, with some being subjected, by force, to some of the most heinous colognes ever conceived.

NANOOKEY OF THE NORTH

These revelations were shocking and tragic. Cynthia Hymen of Pittsburgh reported that her husband tied her to the couch and then forced her to watch a porno film about a family of eskimos and a small walrus called "Nanookey of the North." Deborah Blanchard, a stenographer, told us that her boyfriend Ken was so unsavory that a co-op board had recently turned down his application for a one bedroom apartment—in Beirut.

But of all the women we spoke to, one poor soul stands out in particular. For there was no doubt that she lived in mortal fear of her husband, a maniac named Fred Turner, whose mission in life was to decolorize every film made in the past forty years and turn them black and white. Here is her story:

CONFESSIONS OF A BATTERED WIFE!

"I tried hiding it from my children, my neighbors, even my mother and father, but soon everyone was beginning to notice that I was a battered wife. As I recall, the situation was getting so bad that my husband was battering me two, maybe three times a day, forcing me to sit in a large mixing bowl while he added eggs, milk, and some flour.

"It was humiliating. The way he called me his little "Flapjack." But what was I to do? I depended on him for emotional, financial, and yes, even arch support. I'm so furious at him! He's waffled on every promise he's ever made to me."

THE FRENCH TOAST OF THE TOWN

"Oh yes, in the beginning we were the French Toast of the town. But little did I realize what he meant when he said that he preferred to see me in pancake make-up. "Luckily, the police caught him one night as he was chasing me down the street with an eggbeater. It was the turning point in his life. Fred went into therapy and learned to redirect his hostilities. Now he just batters shrimp, thank God!"

Battered wife.

ART DECO, ART NOVEAU, AND ART CARNEY

Of course, in the real world a man who should hate himself is often not that easy to spot. Vincent was such a man. An avid art collector, he had Art Deco hung in his living room, Art Nouveau hung in his dining room, and Art Carney hung in the bathroom. Yet in and of itself, this was no great insight into the type of man he really was. However, to the trained eye, there were some obvious clues revealing his perverse state of mind.

MATZOH BALLS, CHICKEN LIVERS, AND SMALL SLIVERS OF RABBIS.

Most revealing of these was the choice of aquatic creatures he kept in his private study. In one large tank he had piranha's from the Amazon and in another one, he had an amazing collection of fighting gefilte fish from Israel. They were frightening little demons that would fight voraciously over matzoh balls, chicken livers and, in particular, small slivers of rabbis.

A man of untold wealth ($2.47, to be exact, so you see why he didn't like to talk about it), Vincent would go to any length to indulge his numerous pleasures. But where did he get his money from? Rumors persisted he had made a killing in the market, but later it turned out that he had merely sacrificed a chicken outside a local 7/11. What everybody seemed to have forgotten was that Vincent was a solitary man, impervious to innuendo, who lived quietly by the sea, alone, in a small cardboard cottage.

DRUGS, CRIME, AND RICKY RICARDO

It was a situation that would have continued unchanged except for Sylvia. She was exceptional woman in every respect and who, despite her poor beginnings, continued to live in poverty. A volunteer at a local welfare clinic, she aided low income people in their constant struggle against drugs, crime, and the morbid obsession they were Ricky Ricardo.

It was there that she met Vincent, for he was also a powerful idealist. A staunch defender not only of the homeless, but of the co-op-less and condo-less as well. Suffice to say, Sylvia found herself in-stantly smitten. Infatuated by Vincent's quiet charm, his inner dignity, plus his delightful habit of yodel-ing just before brunch.

HE PAMPERED HIMSELF ON WEEKENDS

Soon she was his constant companion and soon after that, his wife. She quickly discovered all the wonderful little things that only a wife can. For in-stance, Vincent truly enjoyed pampering himself on the weekends and, by the time Monday rolled around, it was all she could do to pull those diapers off him.

However, beneath their storybook romance, lurked a deep, dark secret. A morbid series of events which started to unfold with a knock on the door, early one Sunday morning.

THE POLICE DIG UP VINCENT'S TERRIBLE SECRET:

"Believe me, the day that the police came and started digging up our back yard, I had no idea of what was going on—no idea of how sick the man I married really was. I remember the inspector in charge of the whole operation was a tough guy, but even he was trembling at the sight of all those dismembered, rotted forms that the police were unearthing.

"One after another they brought them up from the ground, some had been stabbed, others shotgunned, there must have been over thirty of them—boxes of Corn Flakes, Shredded Wheat, Quaker Oats, you name it. Lord how could I face the world again knowing that I, Sylvia Kellogg, had married a Cereal Killer!"

Cereal killer.

A POST-IMPRESSIONIST

It took a lot of therapy and hard work for Sylvia to recover from this traumatic experience but, we're pleased to report, that Sylvia eventually remarried.

This time to a gifted young painter, a Post-Impressionist in fact, who does remarkable canvases depicting the inner shelf life of Post Raisen Bran, Post Grape Nuts, etc.

WHY A WOMAN SHOULD STAND BEHIND HER MAN

Let's face it. A lot of times Men Who Should Hate Themselves require that extra little push. Be it off a bridge—or even off a balcony—to realize how loathsome they really are.

Yet many times a bridge, balcony, or even a conveniently open window on a 747 are just not available and, if they are, there's often long waiting lines before you get your chance. But what about the busy woman who refuses to take a number; who doesn't have the time to just stand around all day waiting to push some guy off a cliff.

Well, we think you'll be inspired by the story of Georgia:

UNDER A LOT OF PRESSURE

"My Gil is under a lot of pressure—about sixty thousand fathoms, if my estimates are correct. I remember the exact moment he went overboard. There was only a split-second to act when he screamed out, "Life Saver! Life Saver!!" So I acted, throwing him a Wintergreen, his favorite flavor.

"But we weren't always at odds. On the whole he was a rather attractive sort and—I guess

I have to admit this—I was easily hooked. Yet for some reason, it was only after he took me out of the net and weighed me that he proposed.

"The first few years were a period of adjustment and I gradually realized that Gil was definitely out of my league. For one thing, I attended a School of Nursing and he, at the same time, a School of Guppys. There were other things as well."

A PEANUT BUTTER AND JELLYFISH SANDWICH

"For even at the most rudimentary social functions he was like a fish out of water, constantly flapping around on the carpet, with the only thing that could calm him down a peanut butter and jellyfish sandwich.

"It became too much. The jerk was always all over me like an octopus and, even after drycleaning, I could never seem to get all that black ink off my blouse. Eventually, I came to the decision that I had to throw him back and I tell you I'm not sorry for what I did. After all, he always did claim to be a man of incredible depth."

LIFE UNDER THE PACIFIC

During a follow-up interview, we were able to get Gil to tell us exactly what his feelings were by baiting him with a few questions. He confessed that life under the Pacific was hard, especially in trying to avoid man-eating sharks, but certainly it was no worse than working for the phone company.

Currently, he's emotionally involved with a piano tuna.

HOW TO RECOGNIZE A MAN WHO DOESN'T HATE HIMSELF

♦   Shows affection for himself, even in public.

♦   Remembers his name in the morning.

♦   Talks to himself a great deal, and even listens to what he has to say.

♦   Not embarrassed to introduce himself to his parents.

♦   Never feels obligated to fake erection.

HOW TO RECOGNIZE A MAN WHO DOES HATE HIMSELF

♦   Obsession with death, dying, and going on single's weekends.

♦   Loss of interest in sex, relationships, plus the David Letterman show.

♦   Tends to sleep more than ten years at a time.

♦   Feels that he's not getting older, only fatter.

♦   Has performance anxiety, even during masturbation.

5

JANE FONDUE'S
"AEROPHOBICS FOR MEN"

Clark Barr, a resident of the Windy City, is so obese that when he wades into Lake Michigan for a dip, he winds up flooding Chicago. Donald Rump, a southern belle ringer, has accumulated so much extra poundage on his rear end that it requires a division of WACs just to spank him.

And Fatso Leibowitz, the man who invented the Full Metal Sports Jacket, is so pathologically chubby that the moment he starts to do the Bossa-Nova, it registers 9.8 on the Richter scale.

MAKING LOVE WITH A FORK LIFT

Make no mistake about it. The wives of these men are plainly disillusioned with their spouses and find it just a little stressful, while making love, to have their husbands raised and then lowered over them with a fork lift.

To alleviate the plight of these women, as well as others who may be concerned that their men are not quite in the shape they should be, Jane Fondue has put together an excellent program. It's specially designed to help gradually increase your man's heart rate—through anxiety attacks— to the point where it stops beating altogether.

GETTING HEART RATES UP TO 380 BEATS A MINUTE

All over the country, men are required to report to exercise classes in which thirty women scream at them all at once, "I want a commitment!" I can assure you from first hand experience, this works wonders and immediately gets their heart rates up to over 380 beats a minute.

To begin with, a beautiful instructor with the face of Ingrid Bergman, the hair of Marilyn Monroe, and the figure of Raymond Burr, leads things off with a series of warm-up exercises and men are wholeheartedly encouraged to stretch their legs, arms, in addition to their credit limits.

HOW TO CONDITION THE HEART —EVEN IF YOU DON'T HAVE ONE

These instructors are all quite well trained and compassionate. They realize that Men Who Hate Themselves have traditionally shunned exercises which condition the heart, because most of these guys didn't have a heart to begin with.

Nevertheless, just to be on the safe side, these same instructors are required to have all the men in the class check their pulses every five minutes—in the unlikely event they still have one.

ADVANTAGES OF AEROPHOBICS

1. Lessens political pressure on aching callouses.
2. Prevents twisted ankle bracelets.
3. Reduces tendonitis, and in some cases, gingivitis.
4. Cuts down on the incidence of Hammer and Sickle toes.
5. Puts podiatrists out of work.

DISADVANTAGES OF AEROPHOBICS

1. Results not immediate.
2. Can take up to 30 seconds for a man to be declared legally dead.
3. 20 seconds to be declared illegally dead.
4. Or 10 seconds, if he's a real prince, to be declared regally dead.

WHAT IF HE'S NOT A "GROUP" PERSON?

But what about the man who's uncomfortable about this kind of group atmosphere? The guy who would prefer not leaving the house because it would require help—from the entire U.S. Army Corps of Engineers—just to slip on his loafers.

Well luckily there's a home exercise program that you can help supervise and administer. It's easy. It's fun. And it's quite effective. Just make sure your man is completely relaxed and in comfortable clothes, with his life insurance paid up.

JANE FONDUE'S "AEROPHOBIC" INSTRUCTIONS TO WOMEN:

A) SAY THE FOLLOWING STATEMENTS SINCERELY TO YOUR MAN.

B) STAND THREE INCHES AWAY FROM HIM.

C) USE A MEGAPHONE.

D) REPEAT TILL HIS EKG RATE IS FLATTER THAN KANSAS.

1. "My parents want to meet you."

2. "To tell you the truth, my last boyfriend was bi-sexual."

3. "Oh those weren't Dramamine, those were my birth control pills."

4. "I'm two months late."

5. "Gee. That's funny. My husband never gets home this early."

6. "I'm in love with you."

7. "I'm really in love with you!"

8. "Boy, am I so in love with you!!"

9. "How come you never say you love me?"

10. "Maybe tonight I could tie you up?"

11. "Honey, my whole family's coming over for dinner. You'll just love them. Ever heard of the Manson family?"

12. "If you'd really like to know my husband's name is Don. Perhaps you've heard of him. Don Corleone."

"My husbands name is Don. Perhaps you've heard of him? Don Corleone."

13. "That's not my G-spot. That's a spot on the carpet."

14. "Your wife and I had a very interesting talk this morning."

15. "So you have a boy who's eight and a girl who's nine. That's wonderful. I'd like to meet them sometime and tell them how much their daddy loves water sports."

16. "Herpes. Syphilis. Gonorrhea. No, guess again."

17. "You're the best I've ever had... this week."

18. "Well, actually, I'm fourteen."

A STROKE OF LUCK

As you can see, from this varied menu, getting a conveniently placed blood vessel to burst in your man's cerebrum is more than a stroke of luck. It takes a certain diligence and planning. All well and good. But at this point, even after you've enlisted your man in an "Aerophobics" program, there is probably still one nagging question that's uppermost in your mind. So let us ask it for you:

"THIS IS ALL GREAT, JANE. BUT HOW DO I TELL IF MY MAN IS DEAD?"

It's simple. Just check the following symptoms and see whether he has any one of them—or all of them, for that matter. OK. You know your man is dead...

1. If the nurses and doctors start playing "Super Mario Brothers" on his heart monitor.
2. If six weeks after eating in an expensive French restaurant, he still hasn't ordered desert.
3. If during sex, he keeps on sliding off onto the floor.
4. If he begins to smell like downtown Calcutta or L.A.
5. If he appears unworried that his unemployment checks are coming to an end.
5. If he's so stiff that he can maintain erection but not a conversation. (well, actually, this could indicate he's alive, too.)
7. If, in the last six months, he hasn't urinated.
8. If he offers no resistance to cleaning the dishes. (This is perhaps the clearest sign of all—author.)
9. If he seems to be attracting an unusual amount of flies.

10. If he's Benito Mussolini, Jimmy Hoffa, or is frequently mistaken for Ronald Reagan.

11. If his ghost appears and and demands transfusions of ectoplasma.

12. If more than 90% of his body is covered with moss.

13. If he doesn't object to your mother staying for the month.

14. If his expression seems almost unchanged after repeated stabbings.

15. If he doesn't whine that he's missing the football game while he's being buried.

16. If living with him isn't quite as bad as it used to be.

EXERCISES MEN WHO HATE THEMSELVES HATE

Chin-ups	Sit-ups
Push-ups	Jogging
Aerobics	Weight Lifting
Rowing	Bicycling
Swimming	Calisthenics

EXERCISES MEN WHO HATE THEMSELVES LOVE

Exercises in futility.

6

PROBING THE MALE LIE-BIDO

The male lie-bido is the part of the brain that is responsible for falsehood, pretension, chicanery, and resumé writing. Recent clinical evidence has clearly identified the male lie-bido as the source of all exaggeration, bravado, machismo, plus, it's the place where the imaginary words "eight inches" originates.

Initially, our research was very extensive and it produced some intriguing results. Fans of George Wallace, for example, appeared to be compelled to tell white lies. In addition, we discovered that many men had a habit of telling trumped up stories, but these guys were easily detectable, particularly if they weren't Donald Trump.

What follows is the case study of a man whose pathological lie-bido became so malignant that it could only be removed during a six hour operation in Geneva by a team of specialists employing the latest technology, plus a few polo mallets.

VOTED "MOST LIKELY TO DECEIVE"

"Back in High School, and I'll never forget this, I was voted 'The Most Likely To Deceive.' Would I kid you? Ha-ha-ha! But it was at the Columbia School of Journalism that I learned my most important lesson: Never let the facts obscure the truth—as you know it.

"Believe me, that changed my life. You believe me? Ha-haha-ha!! Wait, this is the best. I remember I once got sex off this one chic because I told her I only had six months to live. And the dumb broad bought it. Ha-ha-ha! The truth was I only had four months. Ha-Ha-ha-ha!!!!!"

THE COMPOSITION OF THE MALE LIE-BIDO

Physically, the male lie-bido is composed of a lot of nerve cells, and you can be sure, these cells have a lot of nerve. If a chart of a man's brain were superimposed over a map of Los Angeles, the male lie-bido would be found exactly at 2930 Sepulveda Boulevard, right next to "The Temple of Oral Love" (or, for those of you not familiar with L.A., about halfway between Paramount Studios and the offices of the William Morris Agency).

THE AMERICAN MACHO ASSOCIATION

Indeed, astounding new research from the AMA (American Macho Association) has shown the male lie-bido to be an intricate network of neurons, ganglia and blood vessels that, in x-ray photographs, appear to bear a striking resemblance to Richard Nixon and senator Bob Packwood.

But perhaps the best way to understand the intricate workings of the male lie-bido is as follows:

COMMON UTTERANCES OF THE MALE LIE-BIDO (TO WOMEN)

◆ "I'll call you this week."

◆ "I've never felt this way before."

◆ "God, oh God, you're the best!"

◆ "Why haven't I met anyone like you before?"

◆ "Me married? What ever gave you that crazy idea?"

◆ "When I'm with you, I forget about all the others."

◆ "Me? Make a pass at your best friend? Honey, don't be ridiculous, she's not even in your class."

◆ "I'm working late."

◆ "I can't believe it. I never came this fast."

◆ "Well, it's not a huge trust fund, but..."

◆ "Of course, I have to admit, it was a low-budget film, but it did win first prize... at the New Delhi Film Festival."

◆ "Really, I could've sworn you were a model."

◆ "Marriage is the only way, I feel, that two people can really be close to each other."

◆ "You know, I thought about you every minute I was away."

◆ "No, the reason I'm turning the lights off is because it's more romantic."

◆ "I'm not dating anyone else."

◆ "Why should I feel queasy about making love while you're having your period? It's a perfectly natural function."

◆ "Two can live as cheaply as one."

◆ "Honey, she must have mistaken me for someone else that looks like me."

◆ "OK, tomorrow night, I'll cook."

◆ "You're kidding! I thought that was your natural color."

◆ "Listen, even the thought of a homosexual relationship disgusts me."

◆ "This is your daughter? I thought you were sisters."

◆ "Of course, even graduating sum cumma laude from Harvard can't open up all the doors."

"Uh, well, last night my, uh, Mercedes blew an oil ring."

♦ "Really, I'm turned on by the smell."

♦ "Your mother is a great lady."

♦ "I'll do more than respect you in the morning, I'll admire you."

♦ "A condom? But the only person I've had sex with for the past twenty years is my ex-wife."

♦ "So far we've raised about fifteen or sixteen million, but that's just start-up capital. Look, I must be boring you."

♦ "I swear, these magazine subscription guys are really obnoxious. Imagine calling eleven'o'clock at night."

♦ "Honey, you don't have crow's feet."

- "Don't you think I feel as bad as you do?"

- "Did anyone ever tell you how cute you are when you're asleep?"

- "I promise to love, cherish, and even to obey."

COMMON UTTERANCES OF THE MALE LIE-BIDO (TO OTHER MEN)

Naturally, the male lie-bido doesn't only operate with women. It's often activated at "male only" gatherings, such as card games, locker rooms, and top level corporate strategy sessions conducted in adjoining urinals.

During these ritual gatherings, men feel obligated to expand upon the events of the previous evening—with some exaggeration, of course. For example, the man who says, "She made my blood boil" may only be referring to the fact that she stuck his head in the microwave. Here are some other common utterances:

- "Yeah, I know I look tired. Must've been those sixteen-year-old twins who were centerfolds!"

- "She must of cum at least eight or nine times"

- "Just like Sophia Loren, only bigger boobs."

- "Sleep? Who got to sleep. Know what I mean, heh, heh, heh, Charlie."

- "Hey, forget about it. She had my pants off the second after I walked in."

- "Then she took the whole thing in her mouth while I..."

- "Listen, I never paid for it in my whole life."

♦ "Are you kidding? I saw parts of Sheila that her gynecologist never even dreamed of checking out."

♦ "Man, she was screaming and moaning so loud I thought I was gonna go deaf."

♦ "So I said, 'Honey please, I have to go to work.'"

♦ "She told me I was even better than Jack Kennedy."

♦ "After I was through doing her, she wanted to pay me."

♦ "I could sell it by the inch or the pound."

♦ "I did the mother and then the daughter!"

♦ "She went down like a submarine."

♦ "All I can say is, she laid miles of pipe in her time!"

♦ "I got souflayed, fillet, parfaid and laid!"

MEN WHO HATE THEMSELVES: BY FAVORITE SEXUAL FANTASY	
Being Totally Dominated	13%
By Green Bay Packers	93%
Having Multiple Partners...	06%
...Of a Law Firm	54%
Animal Sex	50%
With An Understanding Pony	51%
With a Wild and Crazy Wildebeast	97%
Sex With Animal Crackers	52%
Getting Cruelly Whipped	45%
Inside a Blender	128%
Engaging in Group Sex	01%
With In-Laws	99%
Making Love On A Beach	.001%
An Iranian Beach	128%
Six Hours of Mutual Masturbation	72%
With a Mutual Fund Salesman	72.1%
Being Completely Tied Up...	26%
...By Irate Longshoremen	62%
Getting A Light Spanking	05%

7

IMPERSONAL ADS

Men and women searching for just the right person to loathe forever would be hard-pressed—if it weren't for the efforts of a number of single's publications created exclusively for them. One of the most successful of these is "Nerdy In The '90s," a bi-monthly periodical that comes out just once a year.

Editor-in-Chief Clint Westwood found the woman he recently dismembered through just such an ad, and he's eager to share this surefire formula for pain and humiliation with others.

THOSE ZANY, LIVE WIRES

"But you have to be careful," cautions Westwood. "The man who advertises 'Zany, Live-Wire' may just be another one of those crazy electricians. What's more, someone who claims that he's a 'Spirited Man' could be a chronic imbiber of Scotch, Vodka, or even cleaning fluid. Finally, the guy seeking a 'New Lease on Life,' well, the odds are he's probably just been evicted."

Suffice to say, women aren't the only sex

that can be led astray, so can men, and Westwood offers them professional advice as well. "Some women who advertise that " I'm Looking For A Man To Sink My Teeth Into," may not be entirely misleading a man, assuming he's capable of being aroused by a pair of loose dentures. (Just think what her mouth can do with the teeth out...)

WHAT ABOUT THE "COVER GIRL" TYPE?

Likewise the 'Cover Girl Type' could be exactly that, providing the cover is from National Geographic. Yet don't dismiss this type of woman entirely. She may have a lot going for her. Normally you'll find that she's unpretentious and passionate with a certain degree of native intelligence—the kind frequently associated with pygmies.

Also, be cautious of abbreviations. One unfortunate secretary from Des Moines learned only too late that SWM wasn't Straight White Male but, in reality, Sadistic Wichita Minstrel.

What follows is a compilation of "Strictly Impersonal" ads which were scheduled to run in the next issue of "Nerdy In The '90s" had the Editor-in-Chief not been forced, by the magazine's board of directors, into early strangulation.

DOUBLE YOUR PLEASURE:

Siamese twins seek singular man who's not afraid of taking on life's challenges—or our mortgage payments. You cannot afford to pass up this incredible 2 for 1 offer. That's right. We're looking for just the right man to come between us. Romantic type preferred with no present attachments. Call and join us tonight. Actually, we're already joined, so just cum on over!

WILLING TO DATE BENEATH ME:

Suicidal, despondent, psychotic, with MBA, currently living on ledge near top of the Chrysler Building, seeking like-minded distraught female, preferably blond and beautiful, to share last fleeting moments of this unbearable life together. Don't be scared to plunge into a relationship! Tonight—from 78 stories up—let's fall for each other. Smokers O.K. but no acrophobics.

WET AND WILD!

My residence you've probably heard of, Marineland of the Pacific, but there's more to life than just a fancy address. I'm affectionate, warm- blooded, sensual, and can balance a ball on the end of my nose. Lately, all the males I've been meeting seem to belong to the same species, and I wind up getting in over my head. Write to me if you love art, midnight swims, and are a mammal. Children a possibility with advances in science. Waterproof photo a must! Scuba diving equipment a big plus.

ANYONE WHO HAD A HEART:

Would look at me, and know I need a transplant. Seeking a woman who can give me love, tenderness, and her heart forever. I'm sick of all these artificial relationships. I'm ready for the real thing. If you want our hearts to beat as one, don't wait another minute. Write c/o San Diego General Hospital. Hurry! I'll be heartsick if you don't!

PARANOID SCHIZOPHRENIC

I know I'm being persecuted by midgets in rain-coats. And so do I. There are times when I can hear Volvo Dealers mocking my porkpie hat. It makes me feel like doing nasty things. Me too. During the night I can sense life insurance agents, disguised as Nazis, sneaking into my room just so they can soak my arch supports in sour cream. I hate that. Who can blame you? What I seek is an extrovert who loves to walk and—Wait, just you wait a minute. What I want is an introvert who loves to rent mov-ies, cook—Never mind what he says! You have to be between 32-45 and also—Are you out of your mind!? Be 18-21 or get lost! You cradle robber! You necrophiliac! I hate you! Not as much as I hate you!! I could strangle you with my bare hands! They're my bare hands! No they're mine! Take this! Oh yeah! Take that! Take this! That! This!! That!! Arrrrgggghhh!!! By the way, nonsmoker preferred. I totally agree with you.

FED UP WITH BARS?

So am I. What I'm looking for is a savvy, sophisti-cated female, 27-35, who can help spring me from this federal pen. A strong sense of humor and an interest in tennis or skiing are not as important to me as a knowledge of explosives and access to a helicopter. I'm fun-loving, tall and trim, currently serving 25 consecutive life sentences for robbery, murder, and attempted plagiarism of an Emily Brontë novel. Come any Tuesday between 1:00 and 2:00

PM. But please don't wear plaid. It clashes with my stripes.

MATERIAL THINGS MEAN NOTHING TO ME

If they're worth less than $40,000. What I'm looking for is a man whose presence will always be welcome, providing it's gift wrapped. Above all else, I believe that honesty is crucial to a relationship. It's true. I admit that I once turned down Aristotle Onassis' hand in marriage, but only after he didn't offer me the rest of his body. So come on. Let's unite our stocks and options and create a mutual bond. Please include photo, phone number, credit rating and bank balance.

HERPES FREE!

That's right. There's no charge to you. I am a virile male who recently had a blood test and my doctor told me there's absolutely no doubt, I have blood. I can be dominant, submissive, or play the role of Ernest Borgnine, it's all up to you. Believe me there's nothing, absolutely nothing that I wouldn't do to satisfy a woman, except give her pleasure. So don't let a condom come between us. More than anything else, I want to give everything I have to that special someone!

LET'S WOK AROUND THE CLOCK!

Who are you? You are that mystical creature who works right across the street in that Szechuan Laundry. I can see you right through my window because it's late afternoon, and the bus fumes have lifted. Oh, the aromas that waft up to my room every night! The tantalizing smell of sweet and sour shirts, starched shrimps and, my all-time favorite, stir-fried shorts. Dare I mention this? I even know your name. Ling Ring Ding. Yes, my dearest, I could tell immediately that you obviously have breeding—thousands and thousands of roaches breeding in your kitchen right now—but I don't care. Because it's spring. Time to think of life, love, and my special place in the universe, which fortunately is rent-controlled. Yes, we can share it together·and don't worry. By New York standards it's incredibly large. How large? If it were five feet wider, it would be two- dimensional. But we can discuss all that later. Come my little wonton. Come and cover my entire body in duck sauce. That's right. I want the whole neighborhood to hear me scream, "No MSG, oh God, please no more MSG!!!"

COME CELEBRATE THE HIGH HOLY DAYS

And the low holy days. Manic-depressive Rabbi seeks woman with orthodox background in shock therapy. Friends describe me as the "Lennon" type or the "Lenin" type, who knows. Come with me and let's go plant a tree in Israel, if we can find a shovel long enough. Let me tell you, bubby, I'm pretty sensitive, mostly because I got 50% off at my circumcision. Alright, alright, listen. We'll relax, have a drink, maybe even smoke some matzoh together. Believe me, as it says in the Torah, we're all tourists in life until we reach our final destination. Oy, then try getting your luggage. So, if you have over 5000 years of Jewish blood running through your veins, tell me, don't you think it's time for a transfusion?

LET'S GET DIGITAL!

Binary sexual seeks computer mate. You must have over 128K of memory and be available for random access. Looking for a relationship with maximum expandability. I'm IBM compatible and have been told by friends that I've got a great pair of modems. Let's spend the night listening to the magical sounds of Brazilian logarithms. I dislike men who smoke, drink, or use cursor words. Let's exchange data. I can turn your software hard. This baby bytes! No men with terminal diseases or viruses.

MEN WHO HATE THEMSELVES: BY GIRLFRIEND'S BRA SIZE	
38D	01%
48D	001%
58D	00001%
158D	*
36C	14%
34C	24%
32C	34%
22Q	**
34A	67%
28A	76%
1A	***
34B	50%
*Unfortunatly, suffocated to death before he could answer.	01.2%
**Unusual case: Seven breasts, twenty-six nipples, claims her name is Ann Dromeda.	???*
***Boyfriend suffers from acute eye strain.	

8

ZEN IN THE ART OF ANTIPATHY

"A rose by any other name still wilts."
—Gunga Glick

Scientists at the University of Miami have recently discovered, after fourteen years of research, conclusive new evidence of Death after Life. This should come as no surprise to Men Who Hate Themselves, those such as Ned Foyeur, for he is a spiritual being. A believer in the ultimate power and supreme force that rules over the entire cosmos—also known, in some circles, as the IRS.

Here is how his ex-girlfriend Roz Niche tells it:

KARMA MIRANDA AND THE STAGE DELI LAMA

"Jed was strictly into karma. That's Karma Miranda, the famous Tibetan nightclub singer. He'd go out every night to catch glimpses of her at this downtown hangout called the Stage Deli Lama. Strange place. To work there you needed a resume that listed all the employment experience you ever had, including the jobs you held in previous lifetimes—plus references."

380,000 FREQUENT FLYER MILES—AND ALL OF THEM ON ASTRAL PLANES!

"Alright, back to Jeff. Sure he was weird, but I have to admit that I couldn't help admiring a guy who had built up over 380,000 frequent flyer miles—and all of those were on astral planes. That's right. He was a very picky traveler, always insisting on booking special flights that would carry him to pre-destinations."

PURIFYING THE BODY AND DRY-CLEANING THE SOUL

"You know, we just didn't seem to have anything in common anymore and, towards the end, he went out and became a Jewish/Buddhist. He claimed that it was the only holistic way of purifying the body and drycleaning the soul, but I had my doubts.

"As I recall, the last time I ever saw him he was sitting cross legged in the living room, smoking opiated tofu, while chanting, "Hare Knishna Hare Knishna/Cherry Knishna Potato Knishna/Hare Bagel Hare Bagel/Toasted Bagel Cream Cheese Bagel...'

"Well, I think you get the picture."

Jewish Budhist

LSD TRIPS, MESCALINE TRIPS, AND ONE TRIP TO CLEVELAND

Keeping the previous case study in mind, our research has shown that Men Who Hate Themselves are obsessed by trying to achieve that profound and mystical state of decay that occurs only after hundreds of LSD trips, thousands of mescaline trips, or one trip to Cleveland.

All over the country, they're attempting to unite the wisdom of the ancient zen masters with the knowledge of Donald Trump for the purpose of creating a space—and then subletting it.

A STRANGE CASE OF MIND-CONTRACTION

"I started getting into mind-contracting techniques in the late '60s. At that time the movement which was the most popular was PST (Please Stifle Thought). After five hundred dollars and sixty hours without sleep, the one thing I remember was Werner the trainer constantly encouraging us to get off this life/death wheel of karma through quiet mediation and by enrolling in his next seminar, which only cost seven hundred and fifty thousand dollars.

"After that experience, I decided to probe the very boundaries of Cosmic Unconsciousness itself but I eventually gave up—after coming to the music of Barry Manilow."

THE TEACHINGS OF SWAMI BABA GANOUSCH

For centuries Men Who Hate Themselves have been journeying to the temple of the Master himself, Swami Baba Ganousch, in order to absorb his inspirational teachings, while at the same time managing to get away from their wives for the weekend.

For you see, from his shrine high above the river Ganges, the Almighty Seer has proclaimed that what awaits each and every of his disciples is nothing less than Universal Redemption—providing they've also been saving green stamps.

HOW TO REBORN—IN THE ORIGINAL WOMB

To illustrate this point more clearly to Men Who Hate Themselves, the Swami frequently tells a series of parables. Strict adherence to the principles contained within each one, he says confidently, shall produce a wondrous sense of being reborn. For a few men, however, this may occur inside the original womb.

PARABLE #1: ASTRAL REJECTION

A simple woodsman of Braman falls asleep. But while he slumbers his consciousness is suddenly projected up to the ceiling. Looking down at the miserable body of the woodsman, and the miserable body of the woodsman's wife, it thinks better of the arrangement and decides to board a Greyhound bus to Philadelphia.

There it runs for office and becomes Mayor and, soon after that, a shrimp appetizer at a local diner. But six years later the woodsman suddenly wakes up and finds himself in a panic, his forehead drenched in cold beads of tarter sauce.

Looking around his modest hut he gradually steadies his nerves, then promises his wife that he will never again read any more books on Astral Rejection.

PARABLE #2: THE SHE-ELEPHANT

A good physician of Sutra who was old and wise, conversant with the medical arts, and skillful in defrauding Medicare, came home to find that his wife, by accident, had taken a poisonous substance. "Oh Blessed One!" he intoned. "Ask of me whatsoever you wish, but save the one I cherish!"

His prayers were soon answered and his wife died, allowing him to keep a date at the Sheraton with his girlfriend Debbie, a computer programmer.

But later that evening, as she whispered in his ear, "Let me program your software," the spirit of the physician's dead wife appeared in the form of a giant she-elephant, wearing a pants suit.

Stricken with remorse, the good physician fell to his knees and begged for mercy. But the elephant felt no pity for the two lovers and used all her great weight to crush them both to death—though she did resolve, later that week, to go on the Cambridge diet.

LIFE IS A BLIND DATE WITH DESTINY

"As you can see," says the Swami in the most profound of tones. "Life is a blind date with destiny." He then tells all the assembled Men Who Hate Themselves that, to complete their spiritual training, they must make a sacred vow to keep the following zen concepts in their hearts and minds for the rest of their lives, or through the end of the week, whichever comes first.

THE SACRED TEN OF ZEN FOR MEN

1. SCHMATA: A legendary Hindu garment that bestowed immortality, and a small rash, on the bearer.

2. BENIHAHA: The twenty-eighth patriarch of India and the first man to achieve Nirvana by doublecrossing a loanshark.

3. LALA: The void, the ocean of death; the realm of transitory existence, also known as Malibu.

4. SARTRA: A strange existential nausea, said to signal plagues, pestilence, or news of a paternity suit

5. NOOKA: In Buddhist theology, the state of being where eternal oneness is achieved —with Jimmy Hoffa.

6. ZITZBLAH: A joyous philosophy; revelation itself; sacred knowledge based on the eternal truths of "The Beverly Hillbillies."

7. HELLA: After death, a state of misery and eternal anguish, reserved for licensed orthodontists.

8. KOLA: A holy beverage; said to be made from Reincarnation Evaporated Milk.

9. SHABAAS: A three day religious holiday, celebrating a disciple's long ascent to cosmic perfection, ending with the traditional sacrifice of a literary agent.

10. TEENA: A goddess of ancient Burma; the giver of eternal knowledge and, occasionally, a venereal disease.

9

SAFE SEX IN THE '90s (OR HOW TO BE YOUR OWN BEST LOVER)

"Some men want raw sex, others want it steamed."
So says Dr. Baby Ruth, a therapist who specializes
in giving advice to immature men and women, i.e.,
members of the "Baby" boom generation. According to her millions of men and women are turning
off to sex altogether, especially when they're in the
altogether. Yet Dr. Baby Ruth suggests that even
those who choose to remain celibate should take
no chances and always wear a condom, even when
masturbating.

MEN WHO ARE JUST HUNG UP

The facts suggest that the choice to be alone comes
to different people in different ways. Dr. Baby Ruth
explains that she comes across hundreds of men
who continue to be hung up because of a previous
relationship. "Especially if the noose was strong,"
she adds.

She goes on to talk about those men who take
break-ups very badly. Incapable of handling the pain,

they will go out and get themselves thoroughly plastered, sometimes even painted or wallpapered. "Yes, you can die of a broken heart," Dr. Baby Ruth says. "But only if the aorta is involved."

THE CASE OF MILTON DRUBNER—VIETNAM VET

Now we hear from one of Dr. Baby Ruth's most famous cases, Milton Drubner, a Vietnam vet during the Nixon years, who gave shots to almost every poodle in Saigon.

THE PEDERAST WHO WAS PEDICURED

"I've had a lot of problems with my sexual identity. I used to be a pederast but since I went into therapy, I've been pedicured. Still it's tough being a single guy. For awhile I was going out with this lawyer named Sheila, but I never got a chance to sleep with her—even once—because she was always tied up in tubal litigation."

"After that fiasco I got involved with this cocktail waitress, but she was so hyper that she did about 3500 sexual revolutions per minute. By this time I was pretty down on the whole dating scene, but then I met this terrific Jewish girl, Melissa Schtupsky."

"OY VAY! OY VAY! OY VAY!—NOT THAT VAY!!"

> "I remember our first night together and the way Melissa screamed when we made love. 'Oy Vay! Oy Vay! Oy vay!—Not that vay!!' Since that night we've only spoken on the phone, but for some reason she always puts me on hold to take obscene phone calls."

WITHDRAWS FROM WOMEN, SEX, AND NIGHT SCHOOL

Although Milton has now completely withdrawn from women and sex, as well as a Comp Lit course he was taking in night school, he's redirected his energies towards more profitable avenues. Currently, in the area of real estate, he's building a special group of ocean front condos for intellectuals, currently being offered to the public as "George Bernard Shores."

LOVED TO SEND HIMSELF FLOWERS AND CANDY

Dr. Baby Ruth tells us of another one of her cases. A pathological narcissist named Ken who loved himself so much that he often sent himself flowers, candy, and once even an ankle length pearl necklace. Now we hear his story through the words of his last girlfriend:

MORE OF A BOUNTY TOWEL THAN A MAN

"Ken was so self-absorbed that, when you come to think of it, he was actually more of a Bounty towel than a man. It never failed. He loved to catch glimpses of himself in mirrors, store windows, hub caps, particularly those on moving cars. And sexually speaking, he was totally into himself, always forcing me to wear a special mask—one with his picture on it!"

CHOSE TO MAKE LOVE TO HIMSELF

Eventually, he decided that he didn't need a partner and choose instead to make love only to himself. It was pathetic. He would wake up in the morning and say, "Was it good for me too?"

I knew he was on the verge of a nervous breakdown the day he called and asked me if I knew a good lawyer, because he was thinking of slapping himself with a paternity suit."

HAD SEX ORGANS LAMINATED

Unfortunatly, Ken was one of Dr. Baby Ruth's few failures. A conceited egotist to the very end, his will emphatically stated that, for the edification of future generations, he wished to have his sex organs laminated and kept in a large portfolio—a very large portfolio.

THE STRANGE CASE
OF MICK VAH

Next we look into the unusual life of Mick Vah, a drifter who was not only one of Dr. Baby Ruth's former patients, but one of her ex-patients as well.

As it happened, his cousin Bernice decided to throw an Oscar party and it was a wonderful success, despite the fact that only three guests showed up—Oscar de la Renta, Oscar Rubinstein, and 78 year old Oscar Mayer, who walked in holding his wiener.

NOT ONLY COULD BREAK THE
ICE, BUT ARMS AS WELL

Yet this didn't discourage Mick from mingling with his cousin's guests, for he was really quite adept at breaking the ice. It was a social skill that would have been more than welcome had he also not been adept at breaking the rules of grammar, pieces of furniture, as well as several arms.

This show of temper led him to be quickly ejected from the gathering and he found himself on the front lawn, unceremoniously sprawled at Lola's feet.

LUSCIOUS LOLA VICTROLA

Ask anyone who knew her and they would tell you that Lola simply radiated sex, especially after her illicit weekend at Three Mile Island. A scandalous affair, she had been caught redhanded by local church leaders as she attempted to help a muscular young priest celebrate critical mass.

HER BODY HAD MANY DANGEROUS CURVES

But who could blame the poor devil? Lola's body exhibited so many dangerous curves that the state legislature, meeting in closed session, was forced to pass a special law requiring any man who made love to her to wear a seat belt.

So, as Mick rose to his feet, it was this truly glorious feminine vision that filled his eyes. Feeling a rising hunger in his loins, he was instantly enthralled by the mesmerizing scent of Lola's exotic perfume, Eau de Hoboken.

SOMETHING IN THE WAY SHE SMELLS

"Mmmm, the smell of her was soft and beguiling, a fragrance of orchids and lilacs, mysterious, yet not unlike a moonlit night in the midst of a Bombay landfill. What a delicious dish she was! I wanted her to be everything, my mistress, my seamstress, oh I didn't care, any kind of stress would do.

"Curse the cruel fates, curse them I say, for even as I poured out my feelings to her, she told me that her heart belonged to another, although, she added consolingly, her pancreas was still negotiable."

A FEW CRUMBS OF BREAD AND FIFTY MILLION DOLLARS

Mick took her words as rejection and went on a three day bender. However, it ultimately required six uniformed officers to get him to stop bending her. When Mick finally staggered into Dr. Baby Ruth's office, all he had were the clothes on his back, a few crumbs of bread, and direct access to a fifty million dollar trust fund.

INGRID, THE ELEPHANT WOMAN

Seeing the pitiful condition of the dilapidated young man made Dr. Baby Ruth realize that it would take years and years of therapy, meeting with him at least five times a week, before she could afford to make a down payment on the mansion she wanted in Beverly Hills. Indeed, this Mr. Mick Vah reminded her of another one of her famous cases: Ingrid, the Elephant woman, who required three couches just to lie down, but whose ability to pay 1,200 dollars an hour enabled Dr. Baby Ruth to purchase a Leer Jet (a special low-flying plane that allowed everyone on the ground to watch you making contemptuous faces at them).

Realizing she could help this poor, tortured young man finally led Dr. Baby Ruth to accept Mick's case, but only on three conditions: that he promise to attend the sessions regularly, listen to her advice carefully, and pay cash in advance. They began to work together and immediately started making enormous strides. The following is...

A SHOCKING EXCERPT FROM DR. BABY RUTH'S PRIVATE NOTES:

"Today, Mick seemed unusually distraught. He confessed it had been a bad year. A year in which he had lost both his parents. But unfortunatly, someone had found them. Why he hated them so was a mystery to me because they were obviously supportive.

"Early on, they encouraged him in everything he wanted to do, particularly in his desire to throw himself in front of a bus. But—being dyslexic—he kept throwing himself in back of the bus, which made him feel even more of a failure in their eyes."

ATTEMPTED TO SLASH HIS WRISTS

"During one of our sessions, he described in great detail the horrible ordeal he went through when he tried to commit suicide by attempting to slash his wrists—with an electric razor.

Everytime I hear him speak, I realize there are thousands and thousands of therapy sessions that he will ultimately require to reach even a minimal level of functioning, which is great. Because my summer house definitely needs renovating."

26 YEARS IN THERAPY

Miraculously, once Mick was able to break the barrier of talking about his parents, he made an unusually fast recovery which occurred just a few days short of his 26th year in therapy. Even more amazing was that this psychological clean bill of health coincided, to the minute, with the exhaustion of his trust fund.

"The final breakthrough came when I got Mick to see that maybe, just maybe, his father had a right to complain that his work was always piling up on him," notes Dr. Baby Ruth. "After all, the man was a proctologist."

LEARNING TO SPEAK LIKE A REFUGEE

At this point Dr. Baby Ruth shares with us some of the unique insights she's offered through the years, especially to people who want to know how to get their own syndicated TV show.

"A Viennese accent doesn't hurt," she says candidly. "Believe me, I know. For I was born over sixty-five years ago in a seething Ghetto just outside Raleigh, North Carolina, and I sounded even worse than Scarlett 'O' Hara. Let me tell you, it took years and years at the Sigmund Freud Speech Center before I was able to speak like an educated refugee with a Ph.D."

MEN WHO HATE THEMSELVES: BY VISA CREDIT LIMIT	
5¢ or less	100%
67¢	99.9%
99¢	98.9%
$1.00	82.7%
$34.00	71.5%
$102.32	61.5%
$500.00	50.0%
$8401.99	42.8%
$75,000.00	20.0%
$75,001.00	14.9%
$5,361,948.17	08.7%
$49,006,299.99	03.4%
$868,943,736,400.75	01.2%
Over $999,999,999,999,999,999.0	???*
*Michael Jackson refused to comment	

10

DETERMINING A MAN'S H.Q.
(HATE QUOTIENT)

NAME: ARNOLD HANS
AGE: 31
OCCUPATION: PROFESSIONAL LOOKALIKE FOR THE
INVISIBLE MAN

Hates self because he never gets any recognition. Once passed a kidney stone, and it didn't even say hello.

NAME: CECIL MAHLER
AGE: 47
OCCUPATION: CERTIFIED PUBIC ACCOUNTANt

Hates self because his wife Hattie—after twenty years of marriage—continually complains that he can only give her a "Boregasm."

Boregasm

NAME: MAURICE LONGO
AGE: 83
OCCUPATION: UNEMPLOYED DENTIST

Hates self because, for the last 57 years, he's been out of root canal work. Especially misses drilling women patients.

NAME: HARRY KRUTZ
AGE: 29
OCCUPATION: PURVEYOR OF ENVIRONMENTAL MERCHANDISE (UMBRELLA SALESMEN)

Hates self because his wife likes to sleep with a cuddly teddy and the bed gets really crowded—with him, her, and the Senator from Massachusetts.

NAME: DOMINICK SHMUTZER
AGE: 67
OCCUPATION: JUNGIAN THERAPIST

Hates self because he's not as Jung as he used to be.

SHERMAN CAN'T STAND HIMSELF

At first glance, all of these men apparently have confessed to hating themselves, but do they all mean the same thing? Unfortunatly not. For most men have a habit of saying one thing when they mean another. Take for example Sherman Treblinka of Omaha, who recently wrote us and complained that, "I just can't stand myself anymore."

Upon further examination, we found out that all he really needed was just some help getting up.

LOVE, PATIENCE, AND A CATTLE PROD

It was amazing. All it took to gain this wonderful little man's confidence was love, patience, and some occasional jolts with a cattle prod. Sherman, while he was still alive, helped us in learning much. For as precise as our interviewing process was, in a controlled environment devoid of minor distractions, such as food and water, we learned that it was still possible to make errors. What was required was a precise and uniform way to determine—once and for all—how much a man really hates himself—especially in a bathing suit.

FRIENDS, FAMILY, AND PAROLE OFFICERS

That's how HQ was born. It required extensive trial and error, and over fifteen minutes at a local McDonald's, but now here it is. An exam that a man can take in the privacy of his own home, even with friends, family, or his parole officer looking on.

Enough said. Are all you men out there ready to have a truly terrific time as you take a comprehensive in-depth look at every aspect of your life? Then you're taking the wrong test.

CAUTION: After taking this exam, some men might feel as though they're hopeless cases. Others won't be that optimistic.

O.K. Begin.

1. Which gives you the greatest sense of anxiety?
   a) Inflation
   b) Toxic Waste
   c) Nuclear Holocaust
   d) EST Graduates

2. When people first meet you, they treat you with:
   a) Respect
   b) Contempt
   c) Indifference
   d) Thorazine

3. Which is your favorite form of exercise?
   a) Pull-ups
   b) Chin-ups
   c) Sit-ups
   d) Throw-ups

4. At dinner, do you sit :
   a) With your legs apart
   b) With your legs crossed
   c) With your eyes crossed
   d) Under the table

5. What's the last thing you've read?
   a) War and Peace
   b) The Encyclopedia Britannica
   c) Airport
   d) The label on a bottle of sleeping pills

6. The kind of birth control you prefer is:
   a) The pill
   b) A diaphragm
   c) The rhythm method
   d) Not bathing

7. When you know you are right, do you:
   a) Strongly voice your opinion
   b) Logically assert the facts
   c) Gently try to persuade
   d) Apologize

8. You were brought up:
   a) In the city
   b) In a small town
   c) In the country
   d) In a Petri dish

9. What is your major source of income?
   a) Stocks

b) Real Estate

c) Nine-to-five job

d) Check from Mother on your birthday

10. Your best friends would love to see you:
   a) A millionaire
   b) Happily married
   c) On Lifestyles of the Rich and Famous
   d) Dead

11. How do you react to unfair criticism?
   a) Ignore it
   b) Refute it
   c) Disprove it
   d) Agree with it

12. You get others to smile by:
   a) Doing impressions
   b) Telling jokes
   c) Clowning around
   d) Leaving

13. What you most would like to collect is:
   a) Famous paintings
   b) Abstract sculptures
   c) Rare stamps and coins
   d) Dust

14. Complete this famous psychedelic 60's song lyric: "I am you and you are me and we are all_____"
   a) In traction
   b) In trouble
   c) Indifferent
   d) In Cleveland

15. How many miles a day do you jog?
   a) 6000

    b) 10
    c) Less than 1/4 mile
    d) Take a taxi to the bathroom

16. What's your favorite kind of food?
    a) Mexican
    b) Chinese
    c) Lithuanian
    d) TV dinner sucked through a straw

17. The perfect environment for you would be:
    a) A Swiss chalet
    b) A French chateau
    c) An English manor
    d) A Turkish jail

18. Which is closest to your astrological profile?
    a) Libra with Virgo rising
    b) Gemini with moon in Capricorn
    c) Pisces with a double Scorpio
    d) Pisces with a double Hernia

19. If a TV series were based on your sex life, it would be:
    a) The Six Million Dollar Man
    b) Have Gun, Will Travel
    c) Superman
    d) Emission Impossible

20. The type of therapy that would most benefit you is:
    a) Group
    b) Primal
    c) Weekly analysis
    d) Euthanasia

ANSWERS: QUESTIONS 1-20 ARE ALL (SURPRISE) "D." NOW GIVE YOURSELF FIVE (5) POINTS FOR EACH CORRECT ANSWER.

81-100:

Congratulations! Unable to get a new lease on life, you settle for a sublet. In every way your loathing and contempt for yourself is completely justified. As a matter of fact, we've heard there's an excellent possibility that you will be asked to star in "The Geek Tycoon," a film about a shipping magnate who gives up everything for the chicken he loves.

All right, let's face the facts the way they really are. You're a wretched, miserable, abject human being, but not a bad CPA or lawyer.

61-80:

Pretty good. Your feelings about your life tend to vacillate back and forth, alternating between complete shame and total guilt. But on the plus side, thanks to your family's wonderful genes, you'll never lose any of your hair—that is, the hair inside your nose.

What's more, this score reveals that you hate yourself without any reservations, probably because a good hotel wouldn't give them to you anyway. But that's your trouble. You never plan ahead. The only thing you've got saved for a rainy day is $3.42, and a picture of Lorne Greene in a Kimono. Don't worry. We won't ask you why.

41-60:

Not bad. You take a pretty dim view of yourself, which probably results from not paying the electric bill. The only occupation you could possibly find is working as a small time hood—over a Volkswagen engine.

And as if all that wasn't bad enough, you have a tendency to grow petulant, which is often quite difficult, considering the soil and temperature. OK, to sum it all up, in the Great Supermarket of Life, you're standing on the express checkout line.

21-40:

Extremely poor. This score reveals that a lot of work needs to be done. Essentially you're an emotional kind of man, the type who likes opening up completely to a woman, although most would probably prefer not seeing your internal organs.

However, on a more upbeat note, you have been shown to have great distaste for yourself. So much so that, on several occasions, you've gone and had your tongue Scotchguarded.

But don't worry. There's still a lot of hope. Because when it comes to heredity you're right down there, at the shallow end of the gene pool!

0-20:

You're a disgrace! No doubt your positive attitude comes from an overprotective family who, when you were growing up, kept you behind barbed wire. Oh why can't you be a real man who hates himself!? Someone who's not ashamed to stop, take a moment, and smell the mildew.

But no, not for you. You're the type who takes all the vitamins and minerals your doctor recommends and then claims to be completely rejuvenated, even though you weren't Jewish to begin with. It's no use. The odds are completely against you. You'll never ever hate yourself. You're a pathetic specimen!

MEN WHO HATE THEMSELVES: BY COLLEGE MAJOR	
CHEMISTRY	42%
BOTANY	41.7%
ART HISTORY	99.4%
ENGLISH/COMP LIT	99.9%
HISTORY	50.1%
PRE-LAW	17%
PRE-MED	.003%
PSYCHOLOGY	100%
JOURNALISM	101%
BUSINESS	.02.1%
POLITICAL SCIENCE	34.7%
PHILOSOPHY	200%

11

LIVING, LOVING & LOATHING

Most men, according to our survey, said they would love to enter a matrimonial state, just not one with community property laws. Yet when you question them more deeply, you find that almost all of them are cynical, disenchanted and upset, not only with themselves, but with the latest episodes of L.A. Law.

Of course some men only begin to hate themselves after spending an entire weekend with a women, or after spending an entire paycheck, whichever comes first. What we discovered through the course of our interviews was that many men found themselves invaded by a profound sense of sadness, a longing to return to a more innocent time, but generally no earlier than 3:00 PM.

WHY SEX IS MORE TROUBLE THAN ITS WORTH

In another important area there was almost universal accord, because most of the men we interviewed agreed that sex was turning out to be more trouble than it was worth, especially when it wound up costing more than a hundred dollars an hour, plus tip and tax.

The bottom line is what can these men do? Who can they turn to? In our next study, we'll find out:

EDGAR THE FLIRT DOES HIS WIFE DIRT

"Edgar loved to flirt at parties, except he wouldn't flirt with women, only inanimate objects. Often, he'd wink at centerpieces, amuse silverware, and once I even caught him in the cloakroom, fondling a tureen of soup.

"He would claim that his flirtations were innocent and harmless, but after I caught him in a Howard Johnson's under an assumed name, and in the arms of a chair, I knew I could never trust him again."

Caught red-handed in the arms of a chair!

Edgar's wife finally divorced him, some years later, after she found him in a compromising position with a spittoon. He begged her to forgive him—but she would have none of it, preferring instead to spend her remaining years holding hands with a clock.

HE WASHED THAT WOMEN RIGHT OUT OF HIS TOUPEE

This decision crushed Edward, and he wondered about the rationality of his wife, since the clock was digital. But like a lot of men whose wives leave them, in order to cope with the pain and suffering of a failed relationship, Edgar decided to pull himself together and wash that woman right out of his toupee.

Yes, there are all sorts of people who are incompatible, and they always seem to find each other. In the next case study, we focus on a man who loved to immerse himself in relationships, unfortunatly he couldn't swim.

PLAYED STRIP POKER WITH HIS PARAKEET

"When I look back, I don't ever remember Amanda being supportive, except once, before I tried out for the Martha Graham troupe, when she offered to help me into my leotard with a spatula.

"Her sarcasm was really annoying and not only that, she was always reprimanding me. But when she ridiculed me for playing strip poker with my parakeet, that was the straw that broke the camel's back and I really told her off. Well, you know what she did?

"She sidestepped the whole issue and simply said that I looked anemic. 'Oh yeah,' I retorted. 'It just so happens that my parents were born in this country!' I guess that showed her."

THE TWO MAJOR REASONS COUPLES DESPISE EACH OTHER

Sex and money are the two major reasons that couples grow to despise each other, followed closely by money and sex. In the following case study a man and a woman grow increasingly critical of each other, their lives, and certain Swedish movies. What's more, they find themselves subject to the criticism of their children, which is even made more tragic by the fact that they never had any. Hear it directly from the lips of Jerry's wife:

ONLY MADE LOVE EVERY FOUR YEARS

"Our sex life together was becoming pretty infrequent. In fact, towards the end, we only made love once every four years, and even that was just during Presidential inaugurations.

"You know, it was only after we were divorced that I found out that Jerry was having lots of extra-marital affairs, often throwing weddings and Bar Mitzvahs for people he didn't even know.

"Let me tell you it was a nightmare living with him. Mostly because he was so cheap. Once he bought a new copier for the office and you know what, it turned out to be a monk."

WAS PRE-MARITAL SEX THE HEX?

The potential break-up of any relationship is always sad. But when you examine all the issues, perhaps the ultimate cause of Marge and Jerry's problems was the fact that they both strongly believed in having lots and lots of pre-marital sex—only not with each other.

In the professional, workaday world, we found that many men and women just didn't have time to cultivate a relationship. And when they did, often the results were not up to expectations.

THE PHOTOGRAPHER WHO EXPOSED HIMSELF

Take the case of Gregory. As one of New York's top photographers, he experimented with a revolutionary new technique for five years, but was bitterly disappointed when critics suggested that he might achieve more compelling results if he took the lens cap off the camera.

Undaunted, he went out and bought rolls and rolls of film and then proceeded to butter them, until a friend explained that the basic idea was to put the film inside his Nikon. It was a revelation.

115

PERFECT WASP FEATURES

For Gregory always knew that he would become a great and sought after photographer because, and this was his good fortune, he had perfect WASP features, with large antennae coming right out of his forehead.

Because his work was primitive and incomprehensible, he was immediately hailed by SoHo's most prestigious gallery owners as a genius. At one of his gala photography openings, in which he featured film that had been exposed for more than 48 hours (to educational television), he met a woman who was to dominate his thoughts as no other.

A LAWYER NAMED SUE

"What an extraordinary women she was! Over a period of just three months she underwent fifty-seven miscarriages—luckily, they were only of justice.

"Sue, my little Sue, that woman knew exactly how to turn me on! I loved it when she slipped into her legal briefs and paraded in front of me, covering her breasts with flimsy subpoenas, while her voluptuous vulva was provocatively shrouded by sexy show cause orders."

A WELL-HUNG JURY

"Things were so good between us.

"She only objected if I couldn't sustain myself. There I was, all ready to court her, but then the unthinkable happened. She ran off with a well-hung jury. That was the day I decided to give up photography and concentrate on passing the bar.

"But I couldn't pass it, so instead I went in and got drunk."

WHAT BRINGS MEN AND WOMEN TOGETHER

The yearning to find a truly meaningful love involvement continues to bring men and women together, a basic instinct which is only exceeded by that urgent desire to find someone to split the rent with. But some people travel far and wide to find the right person for them, or the wrong person, if it's getting late and the bar is closing down. Such a place is that romantic and legendary retreat that caters exclusively to those men and women who want only to become doctors.

IT HAPPENED AT CLUB PRE-MED

It was there that Paul and Diane met. He had been a "hip" journalist for Rolling Stone, but was summarily fired when it was discovered that he had almost no knowledge of knees, ankles or thighbones. And Diane, she had gotten into medical school through the back door, since her father was the janitor.

On the very first night, they danced. Paul swept her up in his arms and, just a little while later, they sneaked away to take a series of x-rays together.

117

Soon they were exchanging specimens. It was magical.

THEIR STETHOSCOPES INTERTWINED—HOW DIVINE!

Club Pre-Med

"There we were, Paul and me, running free on a nude beach, our stethoscopes intertwined— oh it was too divine! We had our own little oxygen tent on the beach and pina coladas were brought to us regularly by friendly native orderlies.

"But perhaps the most romantic night of all was our last on the island. There we were, under the moonlight, slowly gorging ourselves on bed-pan fried liver, our IV's reflecting the emerald green Caribbean sea. Oh yes, that man could do things with a tongue depressor that would make Masters and Johnson tingle!"

THE PROGNOSIS LOOKS BLEAK

"However, the prognosis for our relationship changed radically when we got back to the states. Because now, before we made love, he had me sitting in his waiting room. At first it wasn't so bad, the waits weren't more than five or ten minutes.

HUMILIATED BY MUTUAL OF OMAHA

"But then I found myself waiting for over an hour and you know what, he was seeing other lovers before me, even though they didn't have an appointment.

"I was hurt. Humiliated even further by Mutual of Omaha, which sent me a form letter stating that I couldn't use my relationship with him as part of the deductible. Finally, I pleaded with him, "How can I ever cure myself of this love I feel for you."

"For a long moment he didn't say anything but instead just looked deeply into my eyes. 'Are you allergic to penicillin?' He asked. The cad!"

LIVES AND AFTERLIVES

Yes, living, loving and loathing, it's been the way of relationships since the dawn of time. You meet someone, you fall in love, and you wind up hating them for the rest of your lives, or the rest of your afterlives, if you're Buddhist.

There's no escape. Sheila Ostrow of Topeka married a guy whose sense of humor was so dry that she had to buy a humidifier. Jeannette Monroe, a weaver of jackets for cocktail franks, wound up with a maniac who treated her like dirt, and who was eventually arrested when he tried to forcibly fertilize the furrows in her brow. The list goes on and on.

BEATRICE, ALFONSO, AND MERV

Beatrice Schnoozer, a distraught young lady, came to us right in the middle of her honeymoon with tears in her eyes and claimed that her husband Alfonso had attempted several times to deflower her while wearing a mask of Merv Griffin.

"Oh why, oh why, is he trying to gross me out!" she sobbed.

We had to shake our heads and confess we didn't know. Maybe it was cheaper by the gross.

MEN WHO HATE THEMSELVES: BY CITY	
Chicago, Illinois	0.34
Secaucus, New Jersey	97%
Little Falls, Arkansas	12%
Newark, New Jersey	97.1%
Hollywood, California	00.2%
Hackensack, New Jersey	98.5%
New Orleans, Louisiana	23%
Hoboken, New Jersey	99%
Fairbanks, Alaska	01%
Trenton, New Jersey	99.7%
New York, New York	50%
Paramus, New Jersey	99.8%
Louisville, Kentucky	39%
Millburn, New Jersey	99.9%
Dallas, Texas	02%
Patterson, New Jersey	0%*
* Yeah, this kinda mystified us too.	

12

PASSIVITY TRAINING
FOR MEN

Are you the kind of man to demand a raise or promotion and get it? Even after you've been fired? Do you return defective jock straps six years later and still get triple your money back? Are you frequently the cynosure of all eyes at cocktail parties because of your wit, charm, and your ability to do fifty push-ups with your tongue?

W.I.M.P. (WOMEN IN MALE POSITIONS)

Small wonder your don't hate yourself, alleges W.I.M.P. organization (Women In Male Positions).

You're a powerful and assertive man who knows exactly how to get your own way. And you probably have other bad habits as well. According to WIMP, it's clear that what your require is a good, weak dose of Passivity Training. A program especially designed so that no matter what the situation, any man can act with all the eloquence and forceful persuasiveness of a professional serf.

A SOCIETY WHERE WOMEN ARE TRULY DOMINANT

This is important. Because W.I.M.P. believes that true equality of the sexes can only be achieved in a society where women are totally dominant: And while WIMP is relatively small at the moment (only 215,875,334 members), their numbers are rapidly growing.

Yes, WIMP is an aggressive organization that professes men will not be able to achieve true hatred of themselves until they're subjugated, dominated, and forced to type over 60 words a minute. Recently, the group proposed legislation that would give the electric chair to any man who refused to handle diapers, laundry, or All Temperature Cheer.

THE DEATH PENALTY vs. CAPITOL PUNISHMENT

In all fairness, however, there is a liberal wing of W.I.M.P. who feels that capital punishment is too extreme a punishment for men in these situations and, instead, suggest merely imposing the death penalty.

MEN GIVEN HARD LABOR TILL THEY FINALLY GAVE BIRTH

Furthermore, demands W.I.M.P., if a man didn't have a hot nourishing supper waiting for his wife when she returns home from work, he would automatically be given 25 years to life at hard labor—or until he finally gave birth.

In addition, it would be absolutely compulsory for every man to wear curlers in public, particularly at shopping malls, and no exception would be made for men who were bald, either.

GRACE, POISE, AND STRETCH MARKS

Finally W.I.M.P. insists that $600 billion be set aside for research to perfect a pill that would not only give men incredible grace, poise and sensitivity, but stretch marks as well.

This year W.I.M.P. has developed a specific training program for Men Who Want to Hate Themselves even more, but first this:

THE RIGHTS OF PASSIVITY

1. A man has the right to beg forgiveness for each and every aspect of his behavior, especially when no apology is asked for.

2. A man has the right to submit to the sexual demands made by anybody of the opposite sex at any K-Mart.

3. A man has the right to be fired without appeal. If his employer cannot find a reason for his dismissal, he is obligated to supply her with one.

4. A man has the right to be sold anything by any woman at anytime; if he suspects that he's not being overcharged, he has the right to demand why.

5. A man has the right, in a physical confrontation with a woman, to get beat up.

THE SIX BASIC SKILLS OF PASSIVITY

1. FORGETTABLE ASSERTION
2. SELF-DEPRECATION
3. NEGATIVE ACQUIESCENCE
4. UNSOLICITED REVELATION
5. AUTO-INTIMIDATION
6. ABJECT EUPHORIA

OK. Let's see some W.I.M.P.s teach men the lessons they deserve!

SITUATION #1:

PHIL WALKS INTO THE SHOWROOM OF A USED CAR DEALERSHIP AT EXACTLY 7:30 AM AND IMMEDIATELY SITS DOWN ON A STOOL IN THE CORNER. AT 4:48 PM, HE APPROACHES THE SALESWOMAN.

PHIL: Excuse me.

SALESWOMAN: Yeah.

PHIL: Do you, uh, remember me? (FORGETTABLE ASSERTION)

SALESWOMAN: No.

PHIL: Of course not. I wouldn't expect you to.

SALESWOMAN: Listen, I'm busy. What is it?

PHIL: Nothing. Oh nothing. Nothing really. (AUTO-INTIMIDATION)

SALESWOMAN: It must be something.

PHIL: Well, I wasn't going to even mention it, but about that car I bought here yesterday, it—

SALESWOMAN: Car? Car? What car!?

PHIL: The...uh...tan station wagon.

SALESWOMAN: With the purple racing stripes?

PHIL: That's the one. What happened—and believe me, I still have absolutely no idea of what I did wrong—is that the transmission fell out. (SELF-DEPRECATION)

SALESWOMAN: You boob! You douche bag!

PHIL: I know. I was a fool to drive it out of the showroom.

SALESWOMAN: Now hold on, buddy. You ain't here to claim a warrantee or nothing like that, are you?

PHIL: How could you say such a thing? (AUTO- INTIMIDATION)

SALESWOMAN: You sure.

PHIL: Positive. (NEGATIVE ACQUIESCENCE)

SALESWOMAN: Hmmmmm...

PHIL: Hmmmmm...

SALESWOMAN: Hmmmmm...so you need a new car?

PHIL: Boy oh boy! That's incredible! You hit the nail right on the head! (UNSOLICITED REVELATION)

SALESWOMAN: See that '51 De Soto over there?

PHIL: The one that's burnt out?

SALESWOMAN: Yeah. Ain't she a beaut!?

PHIL: She sure is. (NEGATIVE ACQUIESCENCE)

SALESWOMAN: Come over here. Look at this. No Michelin Radials.

PHIL: Great.

SALESWOMAN: No AM/FM radio.

PHIL: Terrific!

SALESWOMAN: And with this base sticker price, you also don't get these options: a heater, motor, transmission—

PHIL: What about a sun roof?

SALESWOMAN: OK. We won't throw that in either.

PHIL: Don't say another word! It's a deal!! (ABJECT EUPHORIA)

SITUATION #2:

THE BOSS LADY GIVES DAVE A CALL AT HOME ON FRIDAY NIGHT AT 11:59 PM.

DAVE: Hello.

BOSS LADY: You've got to come in tomorrow.

DAVE: But I'm getting married tomorrow. (FORGETTABLE ASSERTION)

BOSS LADY: Is it an emergency?

DAVE: Well, no. (AUTO-INTIMIDATION)

BOSS LADY: That settles that. Who are you marrying?

DAVE: Mildred Slotnick.

BOSS LADY: That slut!

DAVE: The same one. (NEGATIVE ACQUIESCENCE)

BOSS LADY: That broad's a public health menace. She goes down like a submarine.

DAVE: My feelings exactly. (UNSOLICITED REVELATION)

BOSS LADY: I'll tell you one thing, if you marry that tramp, don't even consider coming in Sunday.

DAVE: You're the boss. (AUTO-INTIMIDATION)

BOSS LADY: So that's your attitude, is it? Well, just for that, you're fired. And to offset the losses you've cost me, I'm not paying you your last six month's wages! Now, what have you got to say to that!?

DAVE: Well...

BOSS LADY: Well!?

DAVE: Well, you've been withholding my pay for eight months. (SELF-DEPRECATION)

BOSS LADY: You are some negotiator. I shouldn't allow myself to be manipulated like this but, OK, make it eight months.

DAVE: What a gal! (ABJECT EUPHORIA)

SITUATION #3:

BARRY HAS A MEETING WITH HIS NEXT DOOR NEIGHBOR GLADYS OVER THE BACKYARD FENCE.

BARRY: Afternoon Gladys.

GLADYS: Afternoon, uh, what's your name?

BARRY: Never mind. (AUTO-INTIMIDATION)

GLADYS: Summer'll be here soon.

BARRY: It sure will.

GLADYS: It's gonna get real hot. That's why I hired a contractor to build me a swimming pool right by the fence.

BARRY: Great idea!

GLADYS: There's only one problem.

BARRY: What's that?

GLADYS: Those weeping willows you got over there.

BARRY: The ones over six hundred years old? (UNSOLICITED REVELATION)

GLADYS: Them's the culprits. They interfere with the sunlight coming over my yard. I don't like to swim in the shade.

BARRY: Neither do I. (FORGETTABLE ASSERTION)

GLADYS: So, if it's OK by you, I'm just gonna grab my chain saw and take those suckers down.

BARRY: The sooner the better. (NEGATIVE ACQUIESCENCE)

GLADYS: And you'll pay for the carting away?

BARRY: No problem.

GLADYS: Just one more thing. I don't like the way your house looks!

BARRY: My house? (UNSOLICITED REVELATION)

GLADYS: It's an affront to the neighborhood.

BARRY: You know, I was just telling my wife the same thing. (SELF-DEPRECATION)

GLADYS: So, as a public service, I called my sister's demolition company to level it.

BARRY: Wow! That's terrific!! (ABJECT EUPHORIA)

MEN WHO HATE THEMSELVES: BY FAVORITE PET	
Dog	08%
Hippo	71%
Sheep	47%*
Toad	93%
Aardvark	50%
Cornish Hen	51.5%
Christie Brinkley	00.0000000001%
Muskrat	68%
Amoeba	02%
Pussycat	45%
Hamster	46%
Skunk	97.9%
Viper	98.9%
Rush Limbaugh	99.9%
Mandrill	33.3%
Womandrill	33.3%
Bald Eagle	17%
Curly Eagle	17.1%
Eagle that uses Minoxydil	17.2%
Praying Mantis	85%
Atheistic Mantis	58%
* May hate selves, but they certainly love their sheep!	

13

MEN WHO ARE THEIR OWN WORST ENEMY
(AND OTHERS LESS FORTUNATE)

In her book "The Female Noodnik" Mildred Tata, a radical feminist, concludes that men also have legitimate grievances and should be afforded exactly the same rights as any other decorative object. However, despite her extreme rhetoric, Mildred writes with remarkable eloquence about her own parents whom she compares, quite favorably, to Steve and Idi Amin.

"I didn't always used to hate guys," she confesses in an early chapter. "In fact, I used to like them quite a lot, until I discovered they were also men. That came as quite a shock!"

PRIX-MATURE EJACULATION

Indeed it took years of therapy for Mildred to recover from this early traumatic experience but, on her sixty-seventh birthday, she decided to throw caution to the wind and she accepted a date with a French race car driver. But much to her dismay, the evening was to end in bitter disappointment, after she discovered that he suffered from prix-mature ejaculation.

ALL MY SONYS

Following that debacle, things looked pretty bleak for Mildred, so she came to where most people with bleak lives eventually come—New York City. Seeking cultural enlightenment, she was immediately drawn to the opening of a political drama entitled "All My Sonys."

The story revolved around a greedy Japanese industrialist who is ultimately driven to harikari after being confronted with the fact that, during World War Two, he made defective Walkmans.

Yet the real drama that night wasn't taking place on stage.

Because it was there, during intermission, that Mildred Tata met Tony Aggiada, a New England mafioso, upon whose small and violent life she was to have a profound, if not minimal, effect.

238 POUNDS OF STEAMED MAINE MOBSTER

"Before I met Mildred, I was the best in the racket. I could knock over a bank in fifteen minutes, a trash can in ten.

"Nobody stood up to me.

"As a matter of fact, there was this one wiseguy who had gotten himself engaged and, on top of that, in trouble with the mob too. Well, I had no choice. I had to put out a prenuptial contract on him.

"Yeah, those were the days.

LACK OF CONFIDENCE MAN

"But Mildred changed all that. She made me insecure. So insecure, that my buddies started referring to me as a "Lack of Confidence Man."

"She, with her college degree, checking and rechecking the spelling of each little ransom note I sent. Forcing me to order cement shoes which met the current building codes.

"Yeah, according to her, I was an embarrassment to the human race, lazy, shiftless and cruel, although she once confessed that I made a passible Beef Stroganoff."

20,000 COLLEAGUES UNDER THE SEA

One day, after Tony started extorting money from Mildred's mother (allegedly to produce an autobiographical film called "20,000 Colleagues Under the Sea"), it dawned on her that he would just never change, so she packed her bags and left, moving in the next day with the noted producer of the hit TV series, "Good Morning, Uganda."

And poor Tony, without Mildred's benevolent guidance, he quickly ran afoul of the feds and was ironically shot down outside a local movie theatre. No, the theatre would never play his film.

CHER AND CHER ALIKE

What was showing was a movie starring Sonny Bono as a mad scientist who clones the woman he's always loved. Up on the movie marquis, the title of the film shown out brightly: "Cher and Cher Alike." It was the last thing that Tony ever saw.

However, unlike Tony, some men who are their own worst enemies are seen by many on the outside as altruists. Like Wally Esperanto, an entrepreneur who invented a revolutionary new product for women called the I.O.U.D., which was essentially a birth control device bought on the installment plan.

A millionaire by the age of 21, Wally met Molly, a professional pasteurizer of camel cheese, at a party given by a mutual friend and a few weeks later they moved in together.

A PARTY FOR THE HOMELESS

"Wally was a very concerned type of guy, you know, very charitable. When I first met him he was planning to throw a party for the homeless, although he later gave up on the idea when he realized how hard it would be to send them all invitations.

"He had incredible insights."

BOLEMIC AND YET OVER THREE HUNDRED POUNDS

"When we first started dating, I had already been bolemic for a period of five years, yet somehow had managed to gain over three hundred pounds. It was Wally who taught me that you have to stick your fingers down your throat after you eat, not before.

"So you can see how gentle and sweet he was.

"Listen, I really don't understand what happened, but we kind of drifted apart. So much so that, towards the end, the only way we could communicate was with signal flags.

"Look, I bear the guy no animosity—just some papers from Marvin Mitchelson."

A GREAT SEXUAL APPETITE

Even today, gentleman that he is, Wally only expresses the warmest recollections of Molly. "She had a great sexual appetite," he says fondly. "And always insisted on keeping Raisinets, Oreos and Clark Bars within six inches of the bed. I miss her."

EVIDENCE PROVES NICE GUYS FINISH LAST

Studying the relationships of guys like Wally proved over and over again that nice guys finish last, especially in bed, where they usually finish several days after their partner leaves. In addition to this, further compounding the feelings of mistrust between the sexes, there were several instances we uncovered of women taking advantage of men who were extremely impressionable.

Thelma Dove, one night at a single's party, encountered a young artist so impressionable that she immediately noticed there were literally thousands of people's fingerprints all over his body. Yet for Selma, it was like a dream come true. But allow her to describe the experience in her own words, or if not in her own words, then in someone else's:

A PSYCHO-CERAMIC RELATIONSHIP

"Edgar was perfect for me, I can't deny it, because I had been seeking a man for a long time that I could mold. So first I molded him into a flower vase, then into some pottery, and finally into a statue of Zeus.

"Well our relationship was going along just great until that fateful day, last October, when he fell off the shelf. Hey—what can I say—it was a shattering experience.

"Ever since then moment my life has completely revolved around Edgar's well-being. I've done everything in my power to pick up the pieces but, you know, it's tough living with a broken man."

Men who are their own worst enemy seem to come in all shapes and sizes, although many places seem to be temporarily out of size 9. They can simply be the boy next door, and sometimes even the girl next door—after a discreet operation in Denmark. Still others can possess phenonemal amounts of wealth.

HE COULD RETIRE TOMMORROW—IF HE MOVED TO BANGLA DESH

A powerful international industrialist, who freely confessed being his own worst enemy, recently said to us, "Listen folks, I have all the money I could ever need. As a matter of fact I could retire tomorrow, if I moved to Bangla Desh.

As you can see, it's extremely hard to stereotype this particular category of man, although, oddly enough, it's not that difficult to monotype them.

HIGH-POWERED LOVE OBJECTS

The point is, and this is a difficult issue to confront, that millions of women from every part of the land are finally deciding that their love objects are just not worth it, particularly if they're powered by more than two batteries.

As Sally Mineola, a long time resident of Dallas, phrased it so eloquently last week on the Phil Donahue Show, "I spent my entire life refining him; and now all I have left is a quart of motor oil."

Given all these adverse circumstances, it's amazing that any relationship can get off the ground at all. Yet here and there, we continue to hear of some rather naive men who actually believe they can make a relationship work. Al Bania is one of these:

ESMERELDA GOES AFTER HIS PITCH

"I recall when I first met Esmerelda at the Baseball Hall of Fame. She was witty, vivacious, intelligent, creative and charismatic. What can I say. I guess opposites attract.

"She batted her eyes at me and soon after that, she was batting clean-up for the Yankees. What a throwing arm she had! She was Mickey Mantle, Willy Mays and Reggie Jackson all rolled into one—weighing in at about 945 pounds. "

A REAL SCREWBALL!

"Oh what curves she had! What screwballs! And what a sinker!

"I remember what got her really excited was the prospect of making love in an open field, but only if there were 50,000 fans in the stadium at the same time.

"Looking back, I guess I'll never totally understand why I struck out with her. Maybe I should have used more resin."

MEN WHO BLAME THEMSELVES

It's amazing. Some men will always blame themselves when things go wrong. A teller in Idaho blamed himself for the failure of his last seven marriages, the failure of his bank, as well as the failure of the latest Middle East peace initiatives.

THE WHOLESALE SLAUGHTER OF THE CHEROKEES

This very same man, for some obscure reason, blamed himself for the wholesale slaughter of the Cherokee indians and felt, had he only been there to intervene, that the whole thing could've been done retail.

Now before we conclude, let's see if we can identify some other common characteristics of Men Who Are Their Own Worst Enemy. Here are some initial observations we've made, primarily because these guys wouldn't give us the other letters of their names.

MEN WHO ARE THEIR OWN WORST ENEMIES ARE...

1. TRUE HUMANITARIANS

Again and again, you will observe that their hearts go out to the world, although they never seem to use enough postage.

2. FORMIDABLE GOURMETS

Quite often of the first order (or the second order if the restaurant is out of what they want). Point of interest. They are known to favor rack of Spam.

3. SOMEWHAT AMBIVALENT

There is no doubt that they enjoy beating around the bush, a tendency that George Bush is trying more and more to discourage.

4. MUSICALLY INCLINED

When surveyed their favorite performer, without a doubt, is Felonious Monk (a rogue accordion player currently serving 25 years to life in Sing Sing for murdering an innocent Melody).

5. MATHEMATICALLY GIFTED

Keen on figures, particularly women's, they like to come full circle, multiplying the radius by pi to figure out their sperm count.

6. LITERALLY HERMAPHRODITES

In fact, many claim they get periods once a month—often into sentences which already contain a question mark or exclamation point.

7. IMMENSELY EGOTISTICAL

According to recent studies, they have been known to announce over 327 times a day, "I couldn't have done it without me."

8. YET STRANGELY MODEST

They truly don't believe there's anything wrong with self- deprecation, as long as they don't insult anybody important.

9. CULTURALLY ECLECTIC

Remarkably informed, they will go out of their way to see a rare film, though once in a while they might be persuaded to see one that's well- done.

10. SPIRITUALLY ATTUNED

Not surprisingly, many have attended seminary schools where they were required to take sacred oaths of poverty and chastity (declarations very similar to the ones taken by writers of humor books).

11. EXTREMELY SENSITIVE

On Sunday afternoons, they can be seen strolling in the park where they'll often spot a sparrow with a broken wing. Yet with no hesitation whatsoever, they'll always reach down and make sure to break the other wing.

12. BORN CRUSADERS

Frequently against cults, there are reports of those who have spent years of their lives attempting to deprogram victims of the Moonies, Krishnas, CNN and Beavis and Butt-Head.

13. CONTROVERSIAL SPEAKERS

North to south, east to west, they tend to stir passions wherever they go by virtue of their extremely libertine attitudes—especially towards parking tickets.

14. TRAGIC FIGURES

All but unknown to the general populous, there is a shockingly high mortality rate among those men at health clubs accidently strangled by barbells (a controversial topic soon to be the theme of a major motion picture entitled "Pumping Irony").

15. MIDDLE-AGED

Through our research we discovered that most of them belonged to an exclusive organization called "So Happy I Turned 40!" or, as it's known more commonly, "SHIT-40!"

MEN WHO HATE THEMSELVES: BY FAVORITE MOVIE	
Patton	01%
High Noon	01%
True Grit	01%
An Unmarried Woman	99.888%
Deep Throat	25%*
Midnight Cowboy	50%
The Graduate	50%
Sleepless In Seattle	50%
Casablanca	00.0000031%
Little Caeser	.001%
Little Women	100%
North by Northwest	11%
South by Southwest	11%
East by Eastwest	110%
Friday the 13th	45%
Friday the 13th Part II	46%
Friday the 13th Part III	47%
Thursday the 28th	98.0003%
* Mostly they hated themselves because they weren't in it	17.2%

14

A DAY IN THE LIFE OF A MAN WHO HATES HIMSELF

AM

8:00 Agnes drops by to talk about their relationship.

8:05 Only five minutes go by and already she's boring him.

8:06 Several yawns later....

8:07 Agnes leaves.

8:10 Goes to mirror. Stands in front and ridicules himself.

8:11 Now his body is rid of cules.

8:12 Just what are cules anyway?

8:17 A brilliant idea. Yes.

8:20 He'll mail himself bomb threats.

8:21 Forgets his address.

8:22 Day not starting out well.

8:30 Will nothing go right.

8:31 Or left.

8:32 Not if he doesn't get his wheels realigned.

8:45 Decides he wants a relationship with no strings attached.

8:48 Symbolically burns Agnes' tampex.

9:00 Heartache. Realizes that he has no friends.

10:00 No family

10:01 No clean shirts for tomorrow.

10:15 But manages to keep his appointment with the periodontist.

10:17 They engage in heavy bondage.

10:43 Comes home. Tongue-tied.

10:45 Looks at his hairline in the mirror.

10:46 No wonder his reputation has always receded him.

11:01 Thoughts of Agnes again.

11:02 The time she deflated his football.

11:03 Burnt his baseball.

11:04 Crushed his ping pong ball.

11:05 Gee, what a ballbuster that bitch is.

11:14 Alright. Time to go out and buy the paper.

11:19 Accosted by panhandlers on the street.

11:21 He finally gives in.

11:22 And buys a few pans.

11:30 Back home again. What a life.

11:31 You're alone when you're born.

11:45 Alone when you die.

11:58 And alone when you live in a studio apartment.

11:59 OK. Time for lunch.

PM

12:00 Maalox on a toasted bagel.

12:01 Nausea.

12:02 Vomiting.

12:03 Throwing up.

12:05 Yes, he definitely makes it better than his mother used to.

12:45 Keeps therapist appointment.

12:50 Talks about his father.

12:51 Who got 3-5 at Leavenworth.

12:52 And then 5-10 at Woolworth.

12:55 High School. Good memories.

12:56 Where he excelled at the sixty yard dash.

12:57 The eighty yard question mark.

12:58 Plus he could also draw an exclamation point over three stories tall.

12:59 But no one cared.

1:00 Breaks down and starts to cry.

1:01 Confesses that whiskey is ruining his life.

1:01 Therapist suggests Scotch instead.

1:02 Session over.

1:03 Suddenly feels guilty about his sister. A former professor.

1:18 Visits her at mental institution.

1:19 They stroll along a psychopath.

1:25 She screams "Eureka!"

1:26 Probably because he forgot to shower.

1:15 Is he being too sensitive?

1:27 Closes his eyes.

1:30 Remembers being dumped by Agnes.

1:31 In a Hefty bag.

1:32 The feelings of humilation come back.

1:33 So do most his checks—and his resumés.

1:34 Funny, he never sent any out.

1:35 Kisses sister good-bye.

1:36 Now wait a minute.

1:37 Wasn't he an only child?

1:38 No time to think about that now.

1:53 Grabs a snack at the local diner. Relaxes.

1:54 And dreams of the perfect date.

1:55 The perfect fig.

1:56 The perfect avocado.

1:57 Becomes emotionally involved with a Greek Salad.

1:59   Check comes. Salad is gone forever.

2:03   He'll never see his olive again. Oh well.

2:10   Back to apartment.

2:11   Decides to relieve tension by masturbating

2:12   Arms too short.

2:13   More frustration.

2:14   Goes to bathroom and glances in mirror.

2:15   Squeezes blackhead.

2:16   Stevie Wonder screams.

2:17   Whoops, wrong bathroom.

2:20   What a day, what a day.

2:23   Time to weigh his options.

2:24   They come out to slightly less than a pound.

2:29   Insight. Realizes that he's carrying a lot of emotional baggage.

2:30   The kind not even American (when they're striking) will check.

2:45   Desperation. Experiments with a mood-altering drug.

2:56   Enters another reality.

3:00   Not unlike Buffalo.

3:12   Alright. Alright. Maybe he's not living up to his full potential.

3:19   Further misgivings about his Agnes.

3:20   She's really driving him crazy.

3:21   And it's such a short drive.

3:22   He could probably walk it.

3:24   Must distract his thoughts.

3:26   Picks up book. Sits down and reads about the Vikings.

3:30   Seems that they traveled in vessels with high sterns.

3:31   Usually Dr. and Mrs. Stern, from Chicago.

3:32   Who also provided the Schmorgorsboard.

3:33	Fed up with history.
3:37	A thought crosses his mind.
3:38	But the light is red.
3:39	It gets killed.
3:42	Why is life so unjust?
3:43	We live.
3:44	We die.
3:45	We miss half-price sales.
3:46	Luckily, there's always TV.
3:47	Goes over. Switches on the educational channel.
3:47	Seems to be an opera about some auto transmission guys.
3:48	Carmen.
3:49	Switches off the educational channel.
3:51	Decides to watch film instead.
3:52	A cross between "Wheel of Fortune" and a Woody Allen movie.
3:54	"Vanna and Her Sisters."
3:55	Definitely time to sell TV.
3:57	Agnes calls. This time to really tell him the score.
3:58	Lakers 68, Knicks 74.
4:00	Oh no! Old emotions come back.
4:02	Must bottle up emotions.
4:03	Bottle breaks.
4:04	Loses deposit on bottle.
4:05	Is there no hope?
4:06	Or chance of salvation?
4:07	Or towels in the bathroom?
4:15	Notices he looks a little pale.
4:20	Off to the tanning center.
4:27	Arrives.
4:29	Almost turned into pair of leather pumps.

4:30   Should've looked at Yellow Pages ad more closely.

4:40   Walks back home.

4:44   Surprise visit from old girlfriend.

4:45   So, after all these years, she still carries a torch for him.

4:46   A blow torch.

Twenty years, and she still carried a torch for him.

4:48   Why are relationships always so complicated?

4:49   Not to mention the phone bill.

5:00   Distraught. Tries to blow brains out.

5:01   With a bellows.

5:30   Arms get tired. Really should do more push-ups.

5:31   Still determined. Opens medicine chest.

5:32   And swallows a bottle of sleeping pills.

5:33   Just the bottle, not the pills.

5:34   Can't seem to do anything right. Lies down.

5:35   A reflective moment.

5:37   True, death may be inevitable.

5:38   But it's certainly preferable to a weekend in New Jersey.

5:42   Is there no relief?

5:43   Certainly not in this year's Yankee bullpen.

93:78   Clock must be wrong.

5:53   Snack time.

5:54   Mmmm.

5:55   Mule livers.

5:57   Starts to put socks in alphabetical order.

5:59   What's this?

6:00   Discovers invitation to cocktail party.

6:01   Rush Rush Rush!

6:02   Arrives at cocktail party.

6:03   Spots a woman named Didi Corleone.

6:05   Says to her, "Funny, you don't strike me as Italian."

6:06   So she hits him.

6:07   Leaves party.

6:11   Meets a gal at the bus stop who instantly lifts his spirits.

6:12   And his wallet.

6:13   Maybe he shouldn't have worn the Naugahyde leisure suit.

6:25   Home again. Sulks around the apartment.

6:30   Then the apartment sulks around him.

6:33   Life sulks.

6:47   Now he's desperate. Really desperate.

6:48   Calls suicide hot line.

6:50   Gets put on hold.

7:50   On hold.

8:50   On hold.

9:50   On hold.

10:50   Tells them that he's going to slit his wrists.

10:52   They tell him that's a foolish waste of time.

10:53   He should hang himself instead.

10:54   Time marches on.

10:57   And so does Newsweek.

10:58   The end is in sight.

10:59   Of course. Because he's sitting on a mirror.

11:00   Dwells on the prospect that he's doomed for eternity.

11:01   Unless he gets out of advertising.

11:11   Opens window and yodels Bosnian National Anthem.

11:12   Hit by Serbian rocket.

11:15   Yes, he almost forgot.

11:27   Remembers to circulate petition amongst his neighbors to have himself evicted.

11:30   Suddenly roof collapses.

11:31   Of mouth.

11:32   Well, at least today wasn't as bad as yesterday.

11:39   Agnes calls again.

11:42   She's eloped with a professional soothsayer.

11:43   A man whom she loves because he can only say, "Sooth."

11:50   Oh what can he do!?

11:53   He's repugnant.

11:54   Vile and reprehensible.

11:56   That's right. He has no business living among decent folk.

11:59   Moves to Venice Beach, California.

MEN WHO HATE THEMSELVES: BY FAVORITE AUTHOR	
Sherry Hite	100+%
Gloria Steinem	100%
Betty Friedan	99.9%
Norman Mailor	.01%
Ernest Hemingway	.001%
James Joyce	65.2%
Gore Vidal	62.1%
Truman Capote	62.1%
Tom Wolfe	32.7%
William Shakespeare	51.9%
Edgar Rice Burroughs	02.0%
Jackie Collins	72.3%
John Clancy	21.6%
Erica Jong	84.4%
Woody Allen	*
* Statistically insignificant—has always hated himself.	

15

THE HATE REPORT
(PLUS CHERI HATE'S
HATE MALE)

Has success spoiled Cheri Hate? We tried to ask her, but this was the message we got on her answering machine: "Hello. This is Cheri. If you were really a close friend of mine, you'd have my private number. Good-bye!"

But where does all this arrogance come from?

As you no doubt know, "The Hate Report" is one of the most profound and controversial books to have come out in the past quarter century; for it has already incited women from around the country to march and demonstrate for immediate change, the most radical of which is changing the word "menopause" (clearly a sexist term) to the more politically correct "womenopause."

NUT BOLTS, AND SCREWS!

Throughout her childhood in New York, Cheri was traumatized by an older brother who was a real lunatic. One day, just before he was going to be locked up in an insane asylum, he escaped and a few minutes later raped a terrified women.

Cheri only found out about the incident after taunting classmates showed her the *New York Post* Headline: NUT BOLTS AND SCREWS! It was a mortifying experience to be related to such a person. For years afterward Cheri regrettably found, try as she may, that she could only achieve orgasm with hardware salesmen.

Once we understand this, it's easy to understand how her other attitudes towards sex evolved.

SEXUAL CONGRESS BY TWO THIRDS MAJORITY

> "I feel I have a right to an orgasm and it's a very political question for me. That's why, when I engage in sexual congress, it's always by two thirds majority, with the full senate looking on."

REMOVING THE "VICE" FROM VICE-PRESIDENT

Additionally, since Cheri is opposed to all forms of male immorality, particularly those practiced by men at the highest levels of government, she's now petitioning to immediately have the "Vice" taken out of Vice- President.

CONFRONTING THE ISSUES

All things considered, there's little doubt that Cheri is the kind of women who makes it a big point to confront all the issues. Recently, during a visit to her local newsstand, she went directly over to the magazine rack and confronted an issue of "Life," berated an issue of "Newsweek," and then told the October issue of "Reader's Digest" exactly what she thought of it.

The encounter quickly became extremely volatile and police were promptly called to the scene when she stopped confronting—and started clawing—the swimsuit edition of "Sports Illustrated."

RECLUSE BECOMES LOOSE WRECK

After this incident, Cheri found that her notoriety had grown to such a point that she was being followed around everywhere by paparazzi, and in some cases, mamarazzi. Not having any privacy was taking its toll and she was fast becoming a recluse, although there were those less generous in the press who characterized her condition as being a loose wreck.

So Cheri moved to a high security luxury building on New York's fashionable East Side. And that's where she met Carl.

SHARING WEEKENDS, DINNERS, AND COLD SORES

Carl, her next door neighbor, heard that Cheri was a fabulous lover, mostly because the walls were so thin. They saw each other for the first time on a beautiful spring day in late December. Both of them, feeling a little lazy that morning, were trying to flag down a limo to the laundry room.

However, limos being a little scarce to find indoors, they both decided to throw caution to the winds and share a seat on the bus. Soon, it wasn't long before they were sharing everything, weekends in the country, candlelight dinners and even cold sores. Wherever you went, they were the talk of the town.

SINGLE ALL HIS LIFE—EVEN WHEN HE WAS MARRIED

Carl, who had been single his whole life, even when he was married, was absolutely infatuated with Cheri. He fixed her lamp, her couch, even her cat, and all with one pair of pliers. Yet there was some trouble brewing in paradise.

Disturbing rumors began to circulate in the local newspapers that Carl had CIA and KGB ties. Now that didn't bother Cheri at all, but those ties from Macy's, those were a disgrace.

And while Carl was obviously a man of extraordinary gifts, Cheri soon discovered that he had stolen most of them from orphans. So it soon became quite apparent, as her infatuation diminished, that she was willing to tolerate less and less.

LOVED TO CHECK INTO HOSPITALS—JUST FOR THE FOOD

Now while she wasn't quite ready to say that Carl had no taste, various friends did begin to point out the fact that there was something a little curious about a man who loved to check into hospitals, just for the food.

In addition to this, at various times, Carl was alternatively convinced that his was Solomon, Moses, Einstein, Mel Brooks and sometimes, all four. Various therapists had dismissed the symptoms as merely being a psycho-semitic illness, but Cheri wasn't so sure.

A NEW DIAPHRAGM CREAM— WITH ONLY HALF THE CALORIES!

Still, she tried everything to please him. On a Friday afternoon she went out and bought a new kind of diaphragm cream, one with only half the calories, but Carl didn't seemed to notice. For he was the kind of man who made it a distinct point to repress all his emotions, yet curiously never his pants.

Everyday it seemed as if his psychological condition got worse.

REJECTED HIM IN POETIC FASHION—USING IAMBIC PENTAMETER

Out of nowhere, he developed chronic insomnia. So he purchased a "White Noise" machine that was capable of drowning out the relentless traffic of the city with the sweet lullaby of waves, waterfalls, or the gentle sounds of Mike Wallace, snoring.

Obviously the man was cracking up. Most of the time tension constricted his throat so badly that he could swallow no more than one strand of spaghetti at a time. Clearly, the handwriting was on the wall.

Cheri knew that, in order to preserve her sanity, she would have to leave him as soon as possible and yet, to her ultimate credit, she rejected him in truly poetic fashion—using iambic pentameter.

NEVER WOULD GIVE HERSELF TO ANOTHER MAN

That night she burned everything, pictures, mementos, presents and—having put that dismal, failed relationship behind her—swore a solemn, sacred oath to herself. Never, never, would she ever give herself to another man.

Lend herself, perhaps.

SARA LEE PIES AND SILICONE

So, fueled by the frustration of this experience, and also by several hundred Sara Lee pies, Cheri set out with a new spirit of purpose and determination to make her name even bigger than before—which she did quite rapidly, by having it injected with silicone. That's why today, in major newspapers and magazines across Nicaragua, you can see the results of these efforts in her syndicated column.

CHERI HATE'S "HATE MALE"

Dear Ms. Hate:
Annette, that's the girl I date, and me, that's the person Annette dates, were having a low-key dinner at a Japanese restaurant in our neighborhood that specializes in designer fish: "Gucci Sushi." Anyway, completely out of nowhere, she starts screaming and yelling that I'm a misogynist. Well, I just couldn't believe my ears. Everybody knows how much I love miso soup. Who's crazy? She or I?
Confused

Dear Confused:
You.

—Cheri

Dear Ms. Hate:
I'm a writer myself. Recently, a friend of mine who's a lifeguard a secretarial pool, introduced me to Kathy. She's a terrific gal who takes over 160 words of dictation a minute—with her toes. I believe after many years I've finally found someone who can not only love, cherish and nurture me, but

also figure out how to use the "Spell" command on my word- processing program. Does it sound like I'm her "type" writer?

Sincerely,

Norman M.

Dear Norman:

The only type writer you are is an IBM (Ignorant, Boring Male). Listen pal, don't you remember when <u>we</u> went out!? Don't you think I remember that you had a severe vowel disorder which manifested itself as a spastic semi-colon.

Boy, what a physical mess you were, with your agonizing muscle spasms—which were followed by your oyster spasms and once even a clam spasm when we visited your parents in Coney Island. Damn! I can't believe that I stayed with you for so long. Even now, I still have the punctuation marks you left all over my body!

—Cheri

Dear Ms. Hate:

I'm a bum. A filthy, no-good, rotten bum. But that's not my problem. My problem is that I can only achieve erection in the back of freight cars. Is there something wrong with me?

Fondly,

Johnny Trash

Dear Mr. Trash:

There's nothing wrong with you that's not wrong with every other guy I've ever met. You're a hobosexual—do you hear me!—a hobosexual! A man

who can only get excited by women who are real tramps!!
   —*Cheri*

Hobosexual encounter.

Dear Ms. Hate:
   Wait till you hear this. I found out that my husband Bud has been having an affair for the past sixteen years with three different women. Their names are—are you ready for this—Rose, Lilly and Daisy. What does this sound like to you?
   All My Best,
   Nadine

Dear Nadine:
   Sounds like Floral Sex. Boy, did you marry a lulu. I wouldn't be surprised if the next gal you caught

him with was named Susan—but she'd have to be black-eyed. What is it with this Bud, anyway? I'll bet'ya he's a product of the sixties. A real flower child.

Not to bruise your feelings or anything like that, but my guess is that as you're reading this letter he's probably pollinating some woman named Blossom right now—on top of a flower bed. Look at the bright side, honey. The guy's no shrinking violet. Maybe you can compromise. Work out a floral arrangement, or something.
—Cheri

Dear Ms. Hate:
How can I tell if my girlfriend is frigid?
Embarrassed

Dear Embarrassed:
See, after making love, if your sperm is frozen.
—Cheri

Dear Ms. Hate:
I'm a former Vice-President of the United States and I think I detect some hostility on the part of my wife. Last night, after making love, she turned to me and said, "Bentsen was right. You're no Jack Kennedy." What do you think she meant by that?
Sincerely,
Dan Q.

Dear Mr. Q:
That you're no Jack Kennedy.
—Cheri

Dear Ms Hate:

My boyfriend Cliff is really into rock music, but I mean real rock music, the kind you make with rocks. Yeah, we went down to this rock festival and we heard volcanic rock, sedimentary rock, plus a rock opera by the Rolling Stones. It was totally outrageous.

Cliff bought me a lemon and limestone soda and then we really pigged out on marble cake. There's only one small problem. He really enjoys getting stoned a lot—but usually by angry mobs. To tell you the truth, I'm starting to feel a little petrified of him.

You think there's any future for us?

Very Truly Yours,

Rock Bottom

Dear Miss Bottom:

No. When I was your age, I also went out with a disturbed rock musician who would sing to me, "Granite and Day, You Are The One." First he wanted me to move with him out to Boulder, next he wanted me to come to Pebble Beach and finally, are you ready for this, he told me he was doing a book on the history of music called "Rock Formations," which he planned to write with a chisel. Well, to make a long story short—just like your boyfriend Cliff—this guy was full of schist.

—Cheri

Dear Ms. Hate:

Sometimes I don't know about Bob. We'll be quietly walking down the street when, all of a sudden, he'll scream at the top of his lungs "On guard!"

and start chasing some poor guy down the block with a sword. What kind of psychological problem do you suppose he has?

Concerned

Dear Concerned:
It's obvious. A duel personality.
—Cheri

Dear Ms. Hate

You've got to help me! I've almost given up all hope. Over the last thirty years I've been to England, France, Ecuador, Thailand, Brazil, you name it, even New Guinea. I've traveled the Torrid Zones, the Tropic of Cancer, all the while circling the Equator and exploring every province and precinct on the face of the earth.

That's right. In Kingdoms, Commonwealths, Motherlands and Fatherlands, I've been looking for love. But the search has proven absolutely futile and now I'm at the end of my rope. You've got to give me the answer. I have to know right now. Tell me, oh God, please tell me! Where can I find the true meaning of love!?

Al

Dear Al:
In the dictionary, you shmuck!
—Cheri

MEN WHO HATE THEMSELVES: BY FIRST NAME

Zeke	67%
Lefty	22%
Angelo	02%
Steve	34%
Tom	50%
Dick	51%
Harry	50%
Adolph	91%
Barry	87%
David	00%*
Elvis	17%
Nikita	43%
Oscar	99%
Herman	99.3%
Schlomo	99.9%
Strange, isn't it?	

MEN WHO HATE THEMSELVES: BY WIFE'S FIRST NAME

Doris	46%
Karen	53%
Sheila	48%
Sharon	51%
Murray	1627%

16

THE HIGH SUGAR/LOW ESTEEM DIET
(or How To Cook Your Man's Goose)

Natural, healthy food—food that's high in vitamins, minerals and protein while remaining low in saturated fat—is obviously far too good for the creeps most women are involved with today.

As a matter of fact, in one recent survey, wives proclaimed that they would like nothing better than to see their husbands leave home and run off with a periodontist—unless they lived in France, where women preferred that their man run off with a Perrier-dontist.

SADO-VEGETARIANS

No doubt, this attitude is further aggravated by the fact that the vast majority of French men are also Sado-vegetarians (sexual deviates who can only achieve orgasm after tying up their wives and then spanking a Waldorf salad).

Consequently, given the worldwide proliferation

of fresh vegetables, lean roast beef, and breakfast cereals containing over 99.8% dietary fiber, it's small wonder that any woman in this day and age can provide her man with the essentials of a totally unbalanced diet.

Luckily, thanks to advances made just within the last three thousand years, all these gals have to do is remember one simple nutritional fact of life:

HYPOGLYCEMIA: HOW SWEET IT IS!

Two thirds of all Men Who Hate Themselves have low blood sugar (the other third has low blood saccharin). In medical terminology, this condition is known as hypoglycemia.

Men afflicted with this ailment undergo incredible mood swings and some even become heroine addicts, experiencing an insatiable desire to stockpile the latest issues of Supergirl and Wonder Woman magazines. Others show more insidious symptoms and often become fixated on obscure films, such as Steve Lawrence of Arabia.

MIGRAINES, FATIGUES, AND FRUCTOSE IN DWARFS

How can a man tell if he's hypoglycemic? In order to determine this, he must eat foods high in sugar and then see whether or not he has the following symptoms: migraines, fatigue, plus the inability to say the word "fructose" in the company of dwarfs.

Salvadore Lovehandle, for the past thirty-six

years, has survived on a diet that has consisted entirely of omelets and soufflès made from chocolate eggs, occasionally garnished with sprigs of licorice.

HIS LITTLE "SUGAR"

So not only is Salvadore nervous, exhausted and overweight, but he's also found the time to become emotionally and physically involved with a Milky Way Bar—whom he simply calls his little, "Sugar."

Of course Salvadore is one of the more obvious hypoglycemics. The question is how can a Man Who Hates Himself tell whether or not he's one too? Fortunately, it's quite simple. Just make sure he answers the following questions "Yes" or "No."

1. Do you find that a Ring Ding is the most perfect object in the universe? (With the possible exception of Julia Roberts clad only in lingerie made of of cotton candy.)

2. Would you be willing to "seek out and destroy" any foreign power that threatened to cut off America's vital supply of Oreos?

3. Over the fireplace, do you have mounted the trophy of a chocolate mousse?

4. Every eight hours, for symptomatic relief, must you take two capsules of time-release nougat?

5. Have you ever requested papal dispensation to wed your Twinkie?

IN CASE OF OCCASIONAL LAPSES

Any Man Who Hates Himself, even if he had only one "Yes" answer, should stop whatever he's doing and immediately start pan-broiling a Nestle's Crunch bar. However, even a Man Who Hates Himself will have occasional lapses and attempt to eat food that's healthy and nutricious. This is the time when The Woman Who Truly Hates Him must step in and take charge of the situation. Let him know, quite firmly, you intend to make sure that he sticks to the following dietary plan. What's more, you should remind him, that if he ever has a wholesome meal again you'll have no choice but to discipline him quite severely—with a sugar cane!

Hypoglycemic being disciplined with a sugar cane.

IF HE WANTS	**GIVE HIM**
1. Scallops Champignon; tuna casserole; clams on the half shell.	1. A herring marinated in Bosco (or a Clark Bar in white clam sauce).
2. Beef Wellington; filet mignon; quarter-pound cheesbutgers	2. An ox basted with maple syrup in a bed of Hershey's Kisses.
3. Baked ziti; fettucini Alfredo; chicken Tetrazzini.	3. Angel's hair pasta in chicken creamery glucose; ravioli a la Milk Duds; veal Parmigiani drenched with molasses.
4. Orange, grapefruit or Prune juice	4. A hogshead of Kool-Aid immediately followed by a vat of vanilla/fudge borscht.
5. Steamed mussels in white wine and garlic.	5. Steamed M&M's in white wine and garlic.
6. Grinders; Sloppy Joes; Hero Sandwiches.	6. A peanut-butter and Jell-O sandwich, topped off by a honey-glazed hoagie.

7. Lamb Tikka; Bhuna Gosht.

7. Tandoori marshmellows; Curried Cannolis with chutney.

8. Cocaine.

8. Opiated Marzipan.

9. Chicken Teriyaki; Futo Maki; Yakitori.

9. Freshly sliced tuna and jelly roll; served with a choice of Brownie Tempura or chocolate-chip sushi.

10. Matzo Brei.

10. Gefilte Glacé.

11. Chili con carne; hot tamales; burritos.

11. Enchiladas stuffed with halvah; refried Tootsie Rolls.

12. Peking Duck; Beef Lo Mein; Mooshu Pork.

12. Hot-and-Sour strudel; Stir-Fried Chicken with Reese's Pieces.

MEN WHO HATE THEMSELVES: BY FAVORITE FOOD

Barbequed Chicken	04%
Waffles With Ice Cream	03.9%
Beets	97%
Tuna In Water	97.01%
Lasagna	.000000063%
Meat Ravioli	.000000062%
Cheese Ravioli	.000000061%
Pizza (with mushrooms)	.00000000000
Broccoli	98.6%
Sushi (Deluxe Platter)	34%
Sushi (Regular)	27%
Sushi (a la carte)	23%
Low-Fat Cottage Cheese	89%
TV Dinners	107.92%
Roast Duck au Grand Marnier	02.35%
Lox, Bagels & Cream Cheese	02.35%
Grapefruit	99.999999999

17

GROVELING, PLEADING, WHINING, BEGGING, PLUS OTHER POPULAR SEXUAL POSITIONS

"Most men give their wives multiple orgasms.
Unfortunatly, in multiples of zero."
—Cheri Hate (author of "The Hate Report")

Remember the days when a woman had to be a combination wife, mother, and doormat? Well those days are long gone. Thanks to Women's Liberation, it's now the men who must conform to their wive's lifestyle, especially in the sexual area. Failure to adjust often means banishment to the couch, the basement, or in extreme cases, Milwaukee.

It's a fact. Men just aren't being afforded the respect they deserve. A former Iranian hostage told us of the ordeal he went through when a woman from the CIA debriefed him, and he was left without underwear.

ABOUT THOSE ONE NIGHT STANDS

Wherever you go nowadays, all you hear are countless women complaining that all men seem to be interested in are one night stands, particularly when their bedrooms are too small to lie down in. But examine the issues more closely and you'll see the real problem is not that men are simply grinning and bearing it. The real problem is that so few women want to see it!

In our first case study, we look at the plight of a man who wishes to remain anonymous, but whose wishes we've ignored and who is actually Emmanuel Bleckerman of 1911 Palo Alto Drive, San Bernandino, California, Apt 3C.

Here he tells us of his harrowing home life:

PUNISHED HIM WITH SEX

"Elayne used to punish me with sex. And when she really got fed up, she punished me with her cooking—often forcing me to fall to my knees and prostrate myself before her meatloaf. It was ironic. Because at first I played the dominant male role, intimidating her not only sexually, but often at marbles as well.

"However, as the months went by, I noticed a subtle change in her behavior. Perhaps it was all those Sensitivity Training courses she took with Yasir Arafat, or the way I would frequently catch her trying to reuse postage on letter bombs. You know what, I think the final humiliation came the night I reached for her in the dark and wound up kissing Simon Wiesenthal."

FEAR, HOSTILITY, AND ROBERT REDFORD

Because of fear, hostility, and the increasing suspicion that most men are not Robert Redford, women in astounding numbers are becoming turned off to sex. The situation has become so critical that hapless men from coast-to-coast are going to any lengths to excite them.

HOW HE EVENTUALLY AROUSED HER

"Believe me, I tried just about everything to stimulate my wife's clitoris. I first started trying to read it the works of Voltaire, next those of Edna St. Vincent Millay and even Chaucer. I tell you, after months and months of trying, the only hint of a response I got was when I started reading it sections of "Airport.""

A "RADICAL" FORM OF LOVEMAKING

More and more we're seeing the "Sexual Politics" become a campaign issue in the bedroom. But perhaps no more fragrantly than in the next case study, where we meet one women who insists on what many may indeed call a "radical" form of lovemaking. It's enough to make a true-blooded American see "red!"

OLGA, TROTSKY, AND GORBACHOV

"Olga was always jetting all over the place, to parties in Moscow, Leningrad, Havana, Peking and Hanoi. On our very first date, I recall, she said that she was attracted to me because I had a beard like Trotsky and a forehead like Gorbachov. Yet despite her attraction to me, I soon realized that I would have no chance of sleeping with her unless I made a pledge to destroy the fabric of western civilization, especially if it were polyester.

Well maybe it was the Cuban cigars she smoked, or the way she jiggled that tatoo of Kruschev on her chest, I don't know. All I know is that maybe I wasn't cut out to be involved with a real "Socialist Butterfly."

THE MEANING OF "FIDEL" IN FIDELITY

Unfortunatly, men who become involved with this type of women find out—all too soon—the true meaning of the word "Fidel" in fidelity. So, given this fact, it wasn't long before Olga was running around town with a marxist plastic surgeon who specialized in bun tucks.

THE ENDS JUSITFY THE JEANS

His advertising motto was "The Ends Justify The Jeans," but what he was particularly noted for was his practice of not using anaesthesia. Instead, he would completely numb his patients by showing them excerpts from speechs by Michael Dukakis.

Yet strangely enough, even though he was a died-in-the-wool Stalinist, what gave him more of thrill than anything else in the world was good old-fashioned American basketball. Indeed, when he went to a game, the only time you ever found him sitting down was during the Star Spangled Banner.

HOW TO BE TOTALLY HUMILIATED AND ABUSED

Of course men like this, those who derive some satisfaction out of life, are the rare exception. A significant number of American men are finding that, no matter how unrewarding their relationships are, they still stand a better chance of being totally humiliated and abused if they journey to an exotic land.

SEVEN WIVES AND ONE DIVORCE SUIT

Ronnie Osmond, a Mormon whose seven wives filed a history-making, class action divorce suit against him, decided to skip town and pursue his masochism south of the border.

Originally, he was hired to teach Spanish as a second language to Mexicans, but it took him six months just to get across the meaning of the word "español." Well, that wasn't the Mexican's fault, nor was it the San Andreas fault, it was his fault.

For Ronnie's skills as a teacher were severely limited by the fact that he was totally illiterate (a condition, by the way, which had never proven to be a hindrance during the 42 years he had served as an advertising account executive). Still, he confesses, he would have left Mexico if it weren't for Rita.

TIAJUANA DANCE AND HOLD MY HAND

"Yes my delicious Rita, with her ruby-red lips, jet-black hair, and incredible olive skin, which unfortunatly didn't come pitted. I can still remember the night I spotted her in a Tiajuana cafe—well, to tell you the truth, spotted her fifty dollars during a floating crap game—but no, that didn't matter.

"For the magic of the evening had us completely caught up in its spell. I donned a sombrero and Rita told me that I had everything Cesar Romero had, minus looks and charm.

"Tequila, more and more tequila, soon the cumulative effects were affecting my judgment and I didn't know if I was coming or arriving. Was it Rita in my arms, or Sophia Loren, or perhaps even Leonard Nimoy? I didn't know and I didn't care."

SHE AROUSED HIM—USING A BILINGUAL APPROACH

I carried her to my room, the one over the cafe, and we made love with the TV on. As she expertly aroused me, using a bilingual approach, there was a late night western playing that I'll never forget. The movie was "The James Gang," starring James Earl Jones, James Earl Ray, James Earl Carter, James Earl of Kent and James Earl, as himself. But why even mention that?"

THE WALLS OF HER VAGINA NEEDED PLASTERING

While Rita thrust up and down, looking to bring herself to climax, I could feel the walls of her vagina. They were soft, warm, perhaps in need of a little plastering. Faster and faster, the images blur, I was struggling to breathe, struggling to satisfy her animal desires.

I guess all that excitement was what sent me to into cardiac arrest, but you know what? The hospital refused to set bail. The corrupt bastards!"

RITA HELPS A CHOKING VICTIM TO EXPIRE

Yes it's a grim tale, but not without a happy ending. For when she was last seen Rita was in her favorite cafe, valiantly helping a choking victim to expire. While several years later Ronnie would use these cheap and tawdry experiences south of the border as the basis for writing a long-running Broadway hit, "Morning Becomes Electralux," a play, in the grand tradition of Eugene 'O'Neil, about a small family of Mexican vacuum cleaners.

Of course, we could have said that the show is really cleaning up at the box office but that type of cheap remark is truly beneath us. (Alright, just barely.)

THE MOST WIDESPREAD FORM OF GROVELING AND PLEADING

Next we come to perhaps the most widespread form of groveling and pleading. Albeit, you may not recognize it in all it's clever disguises but it's revealed by the compulsion men demonstrate—in the presence of the opposite sex—to show they have a sense of humor. A forthcoming book, by Steve Klausner (and a certain D.R.) describes this common syndrome in agonizing detail. It's entitled:

"PUNILINGUS (THE IRRESISTIBLE URGE TO COMMIT FOREPLAY ON WORDS)"

In this deeply insightful work, published simultaneously in Borneo and Cambodia, the authors detail a number of things that men say to amuse women, often with humiliating results. Here are some remarks that have been overheard at various cocktail parties:

"That's strange. Your last boyfriend had a sexual emission every time he was in the presence of certain French cheeses. Well, I guess he suffered from Brie-jaculation. Ha-ha-ha!! Not funny, huh?"

"So you were in Detroit and you couldn't find a tampon. Maybe you should of looked for a brand named Mo-tex. Hey where are you going? I was just kidding!"

"You don't say. You first husband tried to do what to your cat? Really? I suppose you could call him one hell of a Purr-vert. Thanks. My sports jacket needed just a dash of red wine."

Purr-vert.

"It took a lot of courage to tell me that. Your father was a notorious voyeur who terrorized the washrooms of Chinese restaurants. Hmm. Guess you'd have to say the guy was a regular Peking Tom. Wait! Wait! Put that chair down!!"

"So big deal. You were going out with this real estate agent who gave you what, a sexual disease. There's nothing to cry about. It was probably only Herpes Duplex. Uh, listen, is that gun loaded?"

"No kidding. Your brother could only be satisfied by twin Swedish cars? That's incredible. They must have been Vulvos. Get it! Sure, I'd love to come over and see your collection of flame throwers."

"Tell me what happened then. You came home and found him in the arms of Jerry Falwell? Well, what were they having, Moral Sex? OK. OK. I'm sorry, OK."

18

MEN LEARNING TO LOVE TO HATE THEMSELVES

- ◆ Peter, a male secretary, can stereotype over 60 people a minute.

- ◆ Mike, a casting agent, specializes in casting iron, fishing rods, and doubts.

- ◆ Jim, a professional flag pole sitter, feels inadequate because he can never apologize for being sorry.

- ◆ Harvey, a jockey, cries himself to sleep ever since his stable relationship broke up, and his beloved left him for a stud who more closely resembled Seattle Slew.

The end of a stable relationship

♦ David, an advertising Creative Director who earns over $365,000, or a thousand dollars a day, was fired when he demanded an extra $1000 during leap year.

NOW WHAT DO THESE MEN ALL HAVE IN COMMON?

Not that they hate themselves, but that they hate themselves for hating themselves. It's a universal dilemma. Yet even more disturbing is that there are men who have hated themselves all their lives but, for no apparent reason, suddenly begin to like themselves and yes, on rare occasions, even love themselves.

Obviously these alien thoughts of self-worth are

185

causing more than a few men consternation and fear. Without proper treatment, these individuals wind up with obsessive feelings of confidence and self-respect so severe that, many times, they may never punish themselves again by watching "Brady Bunch" and "Partridge Family" reruns.

THE AMERICAN INSTITUTE FOR SELF-NEGATION

"It's not easy," says Cleo Boz-Scagglia, Director of the American Institute for Self-Negation. "For most men live in states of quiet jubilation. Over and over again, these guys never stop complaining that they are condemned to live out the rest of their lives in total rapture, knowing only joy, harmony, and the ravages of utter bliss!"

As a professional, objective therapist, Dr. Boz-Scagglia is determined to help men across the country get to the unconscious roots of their happiness. "I believe these feelings of ceaseless elation can be controlled," she said in a recent article. "If not completely eliminated."

The Kennedy Brothers
Behind the Scenes
From SPI Books

SPI BOOKS
A division of
Shapolsky Publishers, Inc.

☐ **THE KENNEDYS:** *Dynasty and Disaster* by John H. Davis. "Every American should read this book."—Liz Smith. "The definitive Kennedy biography."—*Cleveland Plain Dealer.* "An absorbing book."—*National Review.* "The Kennedy saga—all in one volume."—Anthony Summers. "A dramatic and provocative account."—*Booklist*
(ISBN 1-56171-060-1 – $6.95)

☐ **THE RFK ASSASSINATION;** *New Revelations on the Conspiracy and Cover-Up* by Dr. Philip Melanson. "This book will stun you."—Liz Smith. "Meticulous analysis...cogently argued...effectively discredit[s] both the motives of the police and the entire investigatory process."—*Library Journal.* "You can't write off his research."—*Booklist.* Presents a totally credible scenario revealing that Sirhan Sirhan did not act alone.
(ISBN 1-56171-036-9 – $19.95)

☐ **THE MARILYN FILES** by Robert Slatzer. The definitive story of Marilyn's murder, it will shock you. Contains personal details from Monroe's ex-husband, Bob Slatzer, who maintained a close relationship throughout her life. Exhaustive and well-researched analysis of all the circumstances surrounding Marilyn's death. Reveals a wide variety of scenarios, identifies all the possible suspects including RFK and even JFK. With expert testimony to back it up, the book calls for a reopening of the murder case. Surprising new evidence and a stunning final conclusion!
(ISBN 1-56171-147-0 – $5.99)

☐ **HOLLYWOOD'S UNSOLVED MYSTERIES** by John Austin. Here is a compelling exposé of Hollywood's most sinister true-crime cases. A great source of information about Marilyn Monroe, her murder, the Kennedys, Peter Lawford. Also goes into detail about William Holden, Bob Crane, Natalie Wood and much more. Learn how greed, lust and envy drove celebrities to untimely deaths. "Move over, *Hollywood Babylon!* Something here for every film fan."—*Los Angeles Daily News.*
(ISBN 1-56171-065-2 – $5.99)

☐ **PRESIDENTIAL PASSIONS: The Love Affairs of America's Presidents—From Washington and Jefferson to Kennedy and Johnson** by Michael John Sullivan. "Sullivan comes up with fascinating new details."—*New York Newsday.* Another source of information about Marilyn, her untimely death, the Kennedy brothers, and Peter Lawford. This colorful collection will surprise and shock you—but the stories are all verifiably true. "History class was never like this. Now we know where Washington *really* slept."—*New York Daily News*
(ISBN 1-56171-093-8 – $5.95)

☐ **HERE THEY ARE: JAYNE MANSFIELD** by Raymond Strait. Did you know that JFK had a three-year relationship with Jayne Mansfield? Under the pseudonym of "Mister J," JFK made dates with Jayne through the author. Ray Strait, her press agent and constant companion, knows all the intimate details and the real personality behind this audacious, vivacious movie star. "Convincing and straightforward...an unusual book well worth attention."—*Los Angeles Times*
(ISBN 1-56171-146-2 – $5.50)

SPI EXPOSÉS
The Truth Behind the Story

SPi BOOKS
A division of
Shapolsky Publishers, Inc.

☐ **BEHIND EVERY SUCCESSFUL PRESIDENT:** *The Hidden Power & Influence of America's First Ladies* by Alice Anderson and Hadley Baxendale. The power behind the presidency has often been in the hands of the strong and sometimes controversial women of the White House. Here are Nancy, Rosalynn, Jackie, Betty, Bess, Eleanor and others as you've never seen them—making decisions that have changed the life of our country and influencing presidential policies in the boardroom and in the bedroom. (1-56171-089-X – $16.95)

☐ **MORE OF HOLLYWOOD'S UNSOLVED MYSTERIES** by John Austin. John Austin's case file opens again to dish the dirt that Hollywood is made of. Why did "Mexican Spitfire" Lupe Velez die with her head in a toilet bowl? Did Rex Harrison's cruelty push his lover to suicide? Did blonde goddess Jean Harlow's mother cause her to die a painful and unglamorously dirty death or did she die because of her own shameful secrets? These tragic tales and others make John Austin's new confidential file even more explosive than his last! (0-944007-73-2 – $4.95)

☐ **THE ELVIS FILES:** *Was His Death Faked?* by Gail Brewer-Giorgio. The book that caused a sensation among those who loved the King of Rock n' Roll. New evidence makes this book impossible to ignore. The television broadcast of this material with "Incredible Hulk" star Bill Bixby brought this inside story to nationwide exposure. Now you can judge the new facts in the story that hasn't been solved—until now. Can Elvis be dead when so many facts say otherwise? (1-56171-000-8 – $16.95)

☐ **THE RFK ASSASSINATION:** *New Revelations on the Conspiracy and Cover-Up* by Dr. Philip Melanson. New evidence now demands a reopening of the Bobby Kennedy assassination case. The evidence comes from a decade of independent research and from the government's recently declassified files on the case. The author carefully documents the new evidence for a totally credible scenario—revealing that Sirhan could not possibly have acted alone. Contains shocking, credible new evidence. (1-56171-036-9 – $19.95)

☐ **THE MARTIN LUTHER KING ASSASSINATION:** *New Revelations on the Conspiracy and Cover-Up* by Philip Melanson, Ph.D. "After following Melanson's meticulous pursuit of seemingly every lead in the case there can be little doubt in the reader's mind that neither of the two official versions of what happened could have been the whole truth."—*Publisher's Weekly* "A painstakingly documented indictment..." —*ALA Booklist* (1-56171-037-7 – $12.95)

To order in North America, please sent this coupon to: S.P.I. Books •136 W 22nd St. • New York, NY 10011 • Tel: 212/633-2022 • Fax: 212/633-2123

Please send European orders with £ payment to:
Bookpoint Ltd. • 39 Milton Park • Abingdon Oxon OX14 4TD • England • Tel: (0235) 8335001 • Fax: (0235) 861038

Please send____books. I have enclosed check or money order for $/£ _____
(please add $1.95 U.S./£ for first book for postage/handling & 50¢/50p. for each additional book). Make dollar checks drawn on U.S. branches payable to S.P.I. Books; Sterling checks to Bookpoint Ltd. Allow 2 to 3 weeks for delivery.

☐MC ☐ Visa # _____

Exp. date _____

Name _____

Address _____